DISCOURSE

Sara Mills

LONDON AND NEW YORK

First published 1997
by Routledge
11 New Fetter Lane, London EC4P 4EE

Simultaneously published in the USA and Canada
by Routledge
29 West 35th Street, New York, NY 10001

Typeset in Garamond by Keystroke, Jacaranda Lodge, Wolverhampton
Printed and bound in Great Britain by Clays Ltd., St. Ives PLC

British Library Cataloguing in Publication Data
A catalogue record for this book is available from the British Library

Library of Congress Cataloguing in Publication Data
Mills, Sara, 1954–
    Discourse / Sara Mills.
      p. cm. – (The New critical idiom)
    Includes bibliographical references.
    ISBN 0–415–13854–X (alk. paper).
    – ISBN 0–415–11053–X (alk. paper).
    1. Discourse analysis. I. Title. II. Series.
    P302.M55   1997
    401'.41–dc21   97–10848
                                            CIP

ISBN 0–415–11053–X

To Tony, Gabriel and Francis

chpt 2.

Contents

SERIES EDITOR'S PREFACE   IX

ACKNOWLEDGEMENTS   X

1 Introduction   **1**
Cultural theory/critical theory/literary theory   8
Mainstream linguistics   9
Social psychology/critical linguistics   9
Cultural theory and models of discourse   10
Michel Foucault and discourse   16
Literature as a discourse   22
Note   27

2 Discourse and ideology   **29**
Ideology and truth   32
The subject   33
Determinants of discourse   35
Language, discourse and ideology   42
Notes   47

3 Discursive structures   **48**
The episteme   56
The statement   60
The discourse/discourses   61
The archive   63
Exclusions within discourse   63
Circulation of discourses   67
Conclusions   75
Notes   76

4 Feminist theory and discourse theory   **77**
Confessional discourse   80

Discourses of femininity and heterosexuality 86
Access to discourse 97
Discourses in conflict 99
Conclusions 102
Notes 103

5 **Colonial and post-colonial discourse theory** **105**
Othering 106
Challenging othering 118
Psychoanalysis and discourse theory 123
Conclusions 128
Notes 129

6 **Discourse analysis, critical linguistics and social psychology** **131**
Discourse analysis 135
Social psychologists and discourse 143
Critical linguists/discourse theorists 148
Conclusions 157
Notes 158

BIBLIOGRAPHY 160
INDEX 174

SERIES EDITOR'S PREFACE

The New Critical Idiom is a series of introductory books which seeks to extend the lexicon of literary terms, in order to address the radical changes which have taken place in the study of literature during the last decades of the twentieth century. The aim is to provide clear, well-illustrated accounts of the full range of terminology currently in use, and to evolve histories of its changing usage.

The current state of the discipline of literary studies is one where there is considerable debate concerning basic questions of terminology. This involves, among other things, the boundaries which distinguish the literary from the non-literary; the position of literature within the larger sphere of culture; the relationship between literatures of different cultures; and questions concerning the relation of literary to other cultural forms within the context of interdisciplinary studies.

It is clear that the field of literary criticism and theory is a dynamic and heterogeneous one. The present need is for individual volumes on terms which combine clarity of exposition with an adventurousness of perspective and a breadth of application. Each volume will contain as part of its apparatus some indication of the direction in which the definition of particular terms is likely to move, as well as expanding the disciplinary boundaries within which some of these terms have been traditionally contained. This will involve some re-situation of terms within the larger field of cultural representation, and will introduce examples from the area of film and the modern media in addition to examples from a variety of literary texts.

ACKNOWLEDGEMENTS

I am grateful to Tony Brown for many useful discussions of the use of the term discourse, and also for making detailed comments on drafts of this book. John Drakakis, Lynne Pearce and Keith Green also read drafts of the book and made very constructive suggestions. I would like to thank members of the Sheffield Hallam University staff and postgraduate Critical Theory reading group for discussions of Foucault's work and cultural theory in general. Thanks are also due to Judy Simons, Robert Miles, Jill LeBihan, Christine White, Christine Christie, Deirdre Burton and Elaine Hobby for discussions of the ideas within this book.

1

INTRODUCTION

The term 'discourse' has become common currency in a variety of disciplines: critical theory, sociology, linguistics, philosophy, social psychology and many other fields, so much so that it is frequently left undefined, as if its usage were simply common knowledge. It is used widely in analysing literary and non-literary texts and it is often employed to signal a certain theoretical sophistication in ways which are vague and sometimes obfuscatory. It has perhaps the widest range of possible significations of any term in literary and cultural theory, and yet it is often the term within theoretical texts which is least defined. It is interesting therefore to trace the ways in which we try to make sense of the term. The most obvious way to track down its range of meanings is through consulting a dictionary, but here the more general meanings of the term and its more theoretical usages seem to have become enmeshed, since the theoretical meanings always have an overlaying of the more general meanings. The history of the development of the general use of the term has been chequered; if we take even the simplest route through its history we can see a shifting from the highlighting of one aspect of usage to another:

discourse 1. verbal communication; talk, conversation; 2. a formal treatment of a subject in speech or writing; 3. a unit of text used by linguists for the analysis of linguistic phenomena that range over more than one sentence; 4. **to discourse**: the ability to reason (*archaic*); 5. **to discourse on/upon**: to speak or write about formally; 6. to hold a discussion; 7. to give forth (music) (*archaic*)
(14th century, from Medieval Latin. *discursus*: argument, from Latin, a running to and fro *discurrere*)

(Collins Concise English Dictionary, 1988)

discourse: 1. a conversation, especially of a formal nature; formal and orderly expression of ideas in speech or writing; also such expression in the form of a sermon, treatise, etc.; a piece or unit of connected speech or writing (*Middle English: discours*, from Latin: act of running about)

(Longman Dictionary of the English Language, 1984)

This sense of the general usage of discourse as having to do with conversation and 'holding forth' on a subject, or giving a speech, has been partly due to the etymology of the word. However, it has also been due to the fact that this is the core meaning of the term *discours* in French, and since the 1960s it is a word which has been associated with French philosophical thought, even though the terms *discours* and discourse do not correspond to one another exactly. Thus a French/English dictionary gives us:

discours: a) speech; **tous ces beaux discours**: all this fine talk (*pejorative*); **suis moi sans faire de discours**: follow me and no arguing! **perdre son temps en discours**: to waste one's time talking; b) **discours direct/indirect**: direct/indirect speech (*linguistics*); c) discourse: (*philosophical treatise*); **discourir**: faire un discours: to discourse; to hold forth upon; to chat (*pejorative*)

(Collins Robert Concise French Dictionary, 1990)

During the 1960s the general meaning of the term, its philosophical meaning and a new set of more theoretical meanings began to diverge slightly, but these more general meanings have always been kept in play, inflecting the theoretical meanings in particular ways.

Within the theoretical range of meanings, it is difficult to know where or how to track down the meaning of discourse. Glossaries of theoretical terms are sometimes of help, but very often the disciplinary context in which the term occurs is more important in trying to determine which of these meanings is being brought into play. This book aims to try to map out the contexts within which the term discourse is used, in order to narrow down the range of possible meanings. It is largely the constraints that bound disciplinary structures which demarcate the various meanings of the term: when linguists talk of a 'discourse of advertising', they are clearly referring to something quite different to a social psychologist who talks of a 'discourse of racism'.

Yet, even within a particular discipline, there is a great deal of fluidity in the range of reference of the term discourse. Consider, for example, David Crystal's attempt to pin down the meaning of the term's use within linguistics, by contrasting it to the use of the term text:

> Discourse analysis focusses on the structure of naturally occurring spoken language, as found in such 'discourses' as conversations, interviews, commentaries, and speeches. Text analysis focusses on the structure of written language, as found in such 'texts' as essays, notices, road signs, and chapters. But this distinction is not clear-cut, and there have been many other uses of these labels. In particular, 'discourse' and 'text' can be used in a much broader sense to include *all* language units with a definable communicative function, whether spoken or written. Some scholars talk about 'spoken or written discourse'; others about 'spoken or written text'.
>
> (Crystal, 1987: 116; emphasis in original)

Discourse, like any other term, is also largely defined by what it is not, what it is set in opposition to; thus, discourse is often characterised by its difference to a series of terms: text, sentence, ideology – each of these oppositional terms marks out the meaning of discourse. For example, Geoffrey Leech and Michael Short argue that:

> Discourse is linguistic communication seen as a transaction between speaker and hearer, as an interpersonal activity whose form is determined by its social purpose. Text is linguistic communication (either spoken or written) seen simply as a message coded in its auditory or visual medium.
>
> (cited in Hawthorn, 1992: 189)

And Hawthorn himself comments on this opposition between text and discourse:

> Michael Stubbs (1983) treats text and discourse as more or less synonymous, but notes that in other usages a text may be written, while a discourse is spoken, a text may be non-interactive whereas a discourse is interactive . . . a text may be short or long whereas a discourse implies a certain length, and a text must be possessed of surface cohesion whereas a discourse must be possessed of a deeper coherence. Finally, Stubbs notes that other theorists distinguish between abstract theoretical construct and pragmatic realization, although, confusingly, such theorists are not agreed upon which of these is represented by the term *text*.
>
> (Hawthorn, 1992: 189; emphasis in original)

Emile Benveniste contrasts discourse with 'the language system', when he states:

> The sentence, an undefined creation of limitless variety, is the very life of human speech in action. We conclude from this that with the sentence we leave the domain of language as a

system of signs and enter into another universe, that of language as an instrument of communication, whose expression is discourse.

(Benveniste, 1971: 110)

He thus characterises discourse as the domain of communication, but goes on to contrast discourse with history, or story (*histoire*), which is a distinction more finely developed in French than in English because of the use of different past tenses for formally narrating events and representing events within a more oral frame of reference:

Discourse must be understood in its widest sense: every utterance assuming a speaker and a hearer, and in the speaker, the intention of influencing the other in some way . . . It is every variety of oral discourse of every nature from trivial conversation to the most elaborate oration . . . but it is also the mass of writing that reproduces oral discourse or that borrows its manner of expression and its purposes: correspondence, memoirs, plays, didactic works, in short, all genres in which someone addresses himself [*sic*] as the speaker, and organizes what he says in the category of person. The distinction we are making between historical narration and discourse does not at all coincide with that between written language and the spoken. Historical utterance is today reserved to the written language, but discourse is written as well as spoken. In practice, one passes from one to the other instantaneously. Each time that discourse appears in the midst of historical narration, for example, when the historian reproduces someone's words or when he himself intervenes in order to comment upon the events reported, we pass to another tense system, that of discourse.

(ibid.: 208–9)

Because this seems to be such a specific use of the term, many theorists sometimes prefer to retain the French usage, *histoire/discours*, rather than using the English words.

Some theorists contrast discourse with ideology, for example, Roger Fowler states:

> 'Discourse' is speech or writing seen from the point of view of the beliefs, values and categories which it embodies; these beliefs etc. constitute a way of looking at the world, an organization or representation of experience – 'ideology' in the neutral non-pejorative sense. Different modes of discourse encode different representations of experience; and the source of these representations is the communicative context within which the discourse is embedded.
>
> (cited in Hawthorn, 1992: 48)

Thus, when we try to define discourse, we may resort to reference to dictionaries, to the disciplinary context of utterance or to terms which are used in contrast to discourse, even though none of these strategies produces a simple, clear meaning of the term, but rather only serves to show us the fluidity of its meaning.

In order to try to introduce some clarity into the definition of the term, this introduction aims to provide some fairly straightforward working definitions, as they are currently used within different disciplines. However, discourse, as will be readily observed, cannot be pinned down to one meaning, since it has had a complex history and it is used in a range of different ways by different theorists. As Michel Foucault comments:

> Instead of gradually reducing the rather fluctuating meaning of the word 'discourse', I believe I have in fact added to its meanings: treating it sometimes as the general domain of all statements, sometimes as an individualizable group of statements, and sometimes as a regulated practice that accounts for a number of statements.
>
> (Foucault, 1972: 80)

If we analyse this quotation a little, we will be able to isolate the range of meanings that the term discourse has accrued to itself within Foucault's work. The first definition that Foucault gives is the widest one: 'the general domain of all statements'; that is, all utterances or texts which have meaning and which have some effects in the real world count as discourse. This is a broad definition and is generally used by Foucault in this way, particularly in his earlier work, when he is discussing the concept of discourse at a theoretical level. It may be useful to consider this usage to be more about discourse than about a discourse or discourses, with which the second and third definitions are concerned. The second definition that he gives – 'an individualizable group of statements' – is one which is used more often by Foucault when he is discussing the particular structures within discourse; thus, he is concerned to be able to identify discourses, that is, groups of utterances which seem to be regulated in some way and which seem to have a coherence and a force to them in common. Within this definition, therefore, it would be possible to talk about a discourse of femininity, a discourse of imperialism, and so on. Foucault's third definition of discourse is perhaps the one which has most resonance for many theorists: 'a regulated practice which accounts for a number of statements'. I take this to mean that, here, he is interested less in the actual utterances/texts that are produced than in the rules and structures which produce particular utterances and texts. It is this rule-governed nature of discourse that is of primary importance within this definition. Within most discourse theorists' work, these definitions are used almost interchangeably and one can be overlaid on the other.

To make matters even more complex, whilst Foucault's definitions of discourse have been extremely influential within cultural theory in general, he is by no means the only theorist to use the term, and other definitions of discourse often became enmeshed in the general meanings of the term. For example, Mikhail Bakhtin sometimes uses discourse to signify either a voice (as in double-voiced discourse) or a method of using words which presumes authority (this usage is influenced by the meaning of the Russian word for discourse, *slovo*) (Hawthorn, 1992: 48). Within structuralist and post-structuralist theory, the use of the term discourse signalled a major break with previous views of language and representation. Rather than seeing language as simply expressive, as transparent, as a vehicle of communication, as a form of representation, structuralist theorists and in turn post-structuralists saw language as a system with its own rules and constraints, and with its own determining effect on the way that individuals think and express themselves. The use of the term discourse, perhaps more than any other term, signals this break with past views of language.

As I mentioned above, what makes the process of defining discourse even more complex is that most theorists when using the term do not specify which of these particular meanings they are using. Furthermore, most theorists, as I discuss in Chapters 4 and 5, modify even these basic definitions. What is necessary is to be able to decide in which context the term is being used, and hence what meanings have accrued to it. This book is concerned with demarcating the boundaries of the meanings of discourse, and in the chapters which follow I will be concerned with three contexts of usage, broadly speaking, cultural theory, linguistics and critical linguistics/social psychology. But perhaps it may be useful here to sketch out in a schematic way the range of definitions and the contexts within which they occur, before going on to analyse these in more detail.

CULTURAL THEORY/CRITICAL THEORY/ LITERARY THEORY

Influenced largely by Foucault's work, within cultural theory as a whole, discourse is often used in an amalgam of the meanings derived from the term's Latin and French origins and influences (a speech/conversation) and a more specific theoretical meaning which sees discourse as the general domain of the production and circulation of rule-governed statements. A distinction may be usefully made between this general, abstract theoretical concern with *discourse* and the analysis of individual discourses, or groupings of statements produced within power relations. In Bakhtin's work, and also in Roland Barthes' work, however, as I noted above, a discourse can be taken to represent a voice within a text or a speech position. For theorists such as Benveniste, discourse is the representation of events in a text without particular concern to their chronology in real-time (*histoire*/story).

MAINSTREAM LINGUISTICS

For many theorists within mainstream linguistics, the term discourse signifies a turning away from sentences as exemplars of usage in the abstract, that is, examples of the way that language is structured as a system, to a concern with language in use (Brown and Yule, 1983). For others, discourse implies a concern with the length of the text or utterance; thus, discourse is an extended piece of text, which has some form of internal organisation, coherence or cohesion (Sinclair and Coulthard, 1975; Carter and Simpson, 1989). For other mainstream linguists, discourse is defined by the context of occurrence of certain utterances (thus, the discourse of religion, the discourse of advertising). These contexts of production of texts will determine the internal constituents of the specific texts produced.

SOCIAL PSYCHOLOGY/CRITICAL LINGUISTICS

For social psychologists and critical linguists, discourse is used in a variety of ways, but all of them fuse meanings derived from mainstream linguistics and cultural theory. Thus, social psychologists tend to integrate a concern with power relations and the resultant structures of authorised utterances, such as racism or sexism, with a methodology derived from early discourse analysis

(Wetherell and Potter, 1992; Wilkinson and Kitzinger, 1995). Critical linguists such as Norman Fairclough have tended to be similarly concerned with power relations and the way these shape the production of utterances and texts, but his methodology has been influenced by more recent discourse analysis, and he is thus able to provide a more complex model of the way that discourse functions, and the effects that it has on participants (Fairclough, 1992b). This fusion of linguistics and cultural theory has inevitably resulted in an overlaying of the meanings of discourse from both fields.

This book is mainly focused on how Michel Foucault's ideas on discourse have been integrated into various disciplines in different ways. I will now turn, therefore, to a brief discussion of his work, together with a discussion of Michel Pecheux's theorisation of discourse. I then consider the way that literature might be usefully seen as a discourse, drawing on Foucault's work. This will be followed in Chapters 2 and 3 by more detailed examinations of the uses to which Foucault put the term. In Chapters 4 and 5, I will examine the modifications which cultural theorists, particularly those working within feminist theory, colonial and post-colonial discourse theory, have made to his work and the way that they put the term discourse to work in analysis. Chapter 6 then analyses the way that discourse has at the same time had different trajectories in terms of the way that it has worked out its meanings within discourse analysis, critical linguistics and social psychology.

CULTURAL THEORY AND MODELS OF DISCOURSE

Whilst Michel Foucault is one of the theorists most often referred to when discussing the term discourse, as Diane Macdonnell has clearly shown, there are a large number of theorists whose work on the theorising of discourse is important (Macdonnell, 1986). Macdonnell discusses in detail the differences between the definitions developed by Michel Foucault, Barry Hindess and Paul Hirst, and Louis Althusser and Valentin Voloshinov/Mikhail Bakhtin. She concludes that it is the institutional nature of discourse and its situatedness in the social which is central to all these different perspectives. She states: 'dialogue is the primary condition of discourse: all speech and writing is social' (ibid.: 1), and goes on to say: 'discourses differ with the kinds of institutions and social practices in which they take shape and with the positions of those who speak and those whom they address' (ibid.). Thus, a discourse is not a disembodied collection of statements, but groupings of utterances or sentences, statements which are enacted within a social context, which are determined by that social context and which contribute to the way that social context continues its existence. Institutions and social context therefore play an important determining role in the development, maintenance and circulation of discourses. This institutional nature of discourse is particularly notable in the work of Michel Pecheux, and in discussing his theorising of discourse, Macdonnell comments:

> A 'discourse' as a particular area of language use may be identified by the institutions to which it relates and by the positions from which it comes and which it marks out for the speaker. The position does not exist by itself, however. Indeed, it may be understood as a standpoint taken up by the discourse through its relation to another, ultimately an opposing discourse.
>
> (ibid.: 3)

Thus, particularly in Pecheux's work, discourses (here, groups of utterances/texts which have similar force or effect) do not occur in isolation but in dialogue, in relation to or, more often, in contrast and opposition to other groups of utterances. A simple example of this is the way that the discourse of environmentalism has been structured in reaction to government economic and strategic development policies, and also in reaction to ecological disasters. In this sense, the form that environmental philosophies have developed has depended in a large measure on events and discursive frameworks external to it. However, it could equally be argued that government policy is framed precisely in reaction to pressure groups such as environmental groups; therefore, each group will have its discursive parameters defined for it by the other.

A further aspect which all these views of discourse have in common is that they consider discourses to be principally organised around practices of exclusion. Whilst what it is possible to say seems self-evident and natural, this naturalness is a result of what has been excluded, that which is almost unsayable. Thus, for example, it seems self-evident that we should talk about menstruation in negative terms, describing it in terms analogous to imprisonment and cloaking it in secrecy. One has only to look at advertisements for tampons and sanitary towels to feel this discursive pressure. This feels fairly uncontroversial, since many Western women experience menstruation as a burden, as painful and as limiting their normal lives; but the fact that some women's experience ties in with or is conditioned by discursive pressure does not mean that it has some authentic or real existence. This particular view of menstruation and the experience of menstruation is made possible by the fact that other ways of knowing about menstruation have been excluded. This way of looking at the way women's bodies function can be seen to be part of a medicalised discourse of women's health, which categorises such events as childbirth and menstruation as pathological in relation to a perceived male norm (Shuttle and Redgrove, 1978; Laws, 1990). This is not to suggest, as Shuttle and Redgrove have, that women should therefore celebrate menstruation, but rather to call for a recognition of the excluding of any positive appraisal of the way women's bodies function. What feminist theorists have attempted to do in the last twenty years is to question the naturalisation of these dominant discursive structures within which women's health is discussed in order to make those excluded discursive positions available and to gain credence for them.

A further factor which Macdonnell isolates as pertaining to all definitions of discourse is that 'whatever signifies or has meaning can be considered part of discourse' (Macdonnell, 1986: 4). Whilst this may be seen by some as being too wide a definition of discourse, it does emphasise the fact that discourses are not simple groupings of utterances or statements, but consist of utterances which have meaning, force and effect within a social context. As I will show in Chapter 3, statements – the most fundamental building blocks of discourse – are those utterances or parts of text which have an effect. Statements are not the same as sentences, but are those utterances which can be seen to be grouped around one particular effect.[1] Thus, when a judge says 'I sentence you to three years imprisonment', there are a number of these effects. The judge is institutionally sanctioned, and therefore the force of her/his pronouncement is to transform the accused into a criminal and to enforce a particular sentence on that person. Thus, 'I sentence you . . . ' can be regarded both as a statement and as part of a discourse, since such a statement can only have effect if it is uttered within the context of other utterances (i.e., if certain procedures have been adhered to) and if it takes place within an institutional setting (i.e., within a court room, by an appointed judge).

One theorist whose work can usefully be read in conjunction with Michel Foucault's is the Marxist linguist, Michel Pecheux. His work on discourse (Pecheux, 1982) is important in that he tried to analyse the meanings of words and their relations to larger structures without assuming that words and sentences had a meaning in themselves. He conducted an experiment, later termed the 'Mansholt report', whereby he gave students an economics text to read; he told one group of students that it was a left-wing text and the other group that it was a right-wing text. The text itself could be broadly categorised as a middle-of-the-road economics text, but he showed that each group read the text selectively to fit in with the political framing that he had given it.

In this sense, he gives shape to Foucault's work on discourse by giving a concrete example of the way in which discourses shape our interpretation of texts. If we employ a discourse of 'left-wing economics texts' to interpret a text, we will imbue that text with the meanings of the larger framing discourse.

Pecheux's work is important in that he stresses more than Foucault the conflictual nature of discourse, that it is always in dialogue and in conflict with other positions. He stresses the fact that ideological struggle is the essence of discourse structure. Pecheux also makes a useful addition to thinking on discourses, since he is concerned, as are such theorists as Renée Balibar, with questions of access; whilst Foucault tends to deal with a fairly stable notion of access to discourses, Pecheux is concerned that, for example, people who are not privileged within the class system, through lack of access to education, knowledge and familiarity with information networks and capital, are similarly prevented from having easy access to discourses. Thus, although the same language may be spoken throughout a country (this itself is debatable given, for example, the multicultural environment of Britain in the 1990s), there is a sense in which access to those discursive frameworks which circulate in society is not equally available to all. An example of this is the exclusions in operation with regard to who can publish in an academic journal; in theory, anyone can submit an article for an academic journal, but in practice the article will only be published if it submits to the formal rules of the discourse governing the structures contained within academic papers (i.e., it uses the vocabulary and formal language recognised as appropriate for such writing; it draws critically on other academic articles and cites recent publications by other academics; it conforms to the concerns of articles within that particular journal and uses the vocabulary associated with those concerns). However, generally there are other unspoken rules which govern whether an article is published or not, and these are related to whether the writer is employed by an educational institution, whether the writer is known to the editors or referees of the article, and so on. Thus, whilst access to publishing is, apparently, open to all, in fact there are a number of discursive and institutional barriers which limit academic publishing to those people who are employed in academic posts, who know the discursive rules for writing academic articles and who are able to manipulate their own concerns in line with those discursive structures.

Discourses structure both our sense of reality and our notion of our own identity. Pecheux's work is also very useful in that it enables us to consider ways in which subjects can come to a position of disidentification, whereby we not only locate and isolate the ways in which we as subjects have been constructed and subjected, but we also map out for ourselves new terrains in which we can construct different and potentially more liberating ways in which we can exist. The Women's Movement has been important for many women in mapping out new discursive roles both for men and women. These roles are strongly contested by media representations and by the representations which are constructed through people's interactions with stereotypes of all kinds. But this type of critical knowledge has fundamentally changed and re-presented what it means to exist as a gendered subject. Thus, to go back to the earlier example of menstruation, it is clear that feminist writing and action on women's health has enabled menstruation to be talked about within the public domain, and even for women's sanitary products to be advertised on television. Feminist reappraisals of menstruation have meant that advertising no longer stresses imprisonment; in fact, it could be said that the pressures of feminism have resulted in the altogether surreal advertisements for such products as Bodyform and Tampax where menstruating women perform athletic acts (skydiving, swimming, surfing, pushing broken-down cars) which perhaps are not featured in other forms of advertising for products targeted at women. Thus, feminist disidentification with the dominant discourses concerned with menstruation has resulted in changes in the representation of menstruation within the public domain, and ultimately in alternative ways of considering women's health. However, in this instance, the surreal nature of the advertising concerning sanitary products does signal a singular inability to cope with the experience of menstruation – the advertisements are still concerned with the erasing of menstruation, rather than with dealing with more positive views of menstrual periods.

Thus, for Pecheux in particular, discourses do not exist in isolation, but are the object and site of struggle. Discourses are thus not fixed but are the site of constant contestation of meaning.

MICHEL FOUCAULT AND DISCOURSE

> What I have said is not 'what I think' but often what I wonder whether it couldn't be thought.
>
> (Foucault, 1979d: 58)

> Foucault's study begins the immense task of dismantling the theme that knowledge is an expression of men's [sic] ideas.
>
> (Macdonnell, 1986: 86)

Michel Foucault's work has been crucial to the development of a range of different theories which have been broadly grouped under the term 'discourse theory', and it is for this reason that this book will focus primarily on his work. Foucault's work is often difficult to understand, partly because of its sometimes convoluted style and the density of reference he uses. But perhaps, the main reason why Foucault is considered difficult is because, more than any other theorist, he challenges many of the preconceived notions that we have about a wide range of different subjects: sexuality, madness, discipline, subjectivity, language.

I endeavour in Chapters 3 and 4 of this book to draw on some of Foucault's writing which helps readers to think about the term discourse. Foucault does give some general definitions of discourse which I shall discuss in some detail, but perhaps the most useful way to investigate the term is to see how it is used by Foucault in his discussions of power, knowledge and truth, since this configuration is essentially what constitutes discourse.

Foucault's work is not a system of ideas nor a general theory; his work ranges over an extremely wide variety of subjects and it is very difficult to pin him down as a historian, a philosopher, a psychologist or a critical theorist. As he himself says:

> All my books . . . are little tool boxes . . . if people want to open them, to use this sentence or that idea as a screwdriver or spanner to short-circuit, discredit or smash systems of power, including eventually those from which my books have emerged . . . so much the better.
>
> (cited in Patton, 1979a: 115)

Thus, the term discourse is not rooted within a larger system of fully worked-out theoretical ideas, but is one element in Foucault's work. This lack of system sometimes causes difficulty for theorists and may be one of the reasons that there are so many different definitions of the term discourse, and so many modifications of the meaning of the term. However, this lack of general system is also what makes for a certain flexibility when theorists are trying to use Foucault's work to fit changing social circumstances.

One of the most productive ways of thinking about discourse is not as a group of signs or a stretch of text, but as 'practices that systematically form the objects of which they speak' (Foucault, 1972: 49). In this sense, a discourse is something which produces something else (an utterance, a concept, an effect), rather than something which exists in and of itself and which can be analysed in isolation. A discursive structure can be detected because of the systematicity of the ideas, opinions, concepts, ways of thinking and behaving which are formed within a particular context, and because of the effects of those ways of thinking and behaving. Thus, we can assume that there is a set of discourses of femininity and masculinity, because women and men behave within a certain range of parameters when defining themselves as gendered subjects. These discursive frameworks demarcate the boundaries within which we can negotiate what it means to be gendered. It is these discourses which heterosexual, lesbian, gay, bisexual and transsexual/transvestite subjects engage with when coming to understand themselves as sexed: when a lesbian takes up a 'femme' position, it is her perception of the discourse of heterosexual femininity that she is actively modifying and reworking and ultimately destabilising (Bell, *et al.*, 1994). This discursive framework of femininity may determine the types of clothes she chooses to wear, the types of bodily stance she adopts and ways of thinking about herself and others in relation to power.

In terms of thinking about discourse as having effects, it is important to consider the factors of truth, power and knowledge, since it is because of these elements that discourse has effects. Truth, for Foucault, is not something intrinsic to an utterance, nor is it an ideal abstract quality to which humans aspire; he sees truth as being something far more worldly and more negative:

> Truth is of the world; it is produced there by virtue of multiple constraints. . . . Each society has its regime of truth, its 'general politics' of truth: that is the types of discourse it harbours and causes to function as true: the mechanisms and instances which enable one to distinguish true from false statements, the way in which each is sanctioned; the techniques and procedures which are valorised for obtaining truth: the status of those who are charged with saying what counts as true.
>
> (Foucault, 1979e: 46)

Truth, therefore, is something which societies have to work to produce, rather than something which appears in a transcendental way. Foucault analyses the labour which people perform to exclude certain forms of knowledge from consideration as 'true'. To consider an example which Norman Fairclough discusses (Fairclough 1992b), 'alternative' knowledge about health is not given the same status as conventional medical science; a great deal of effort and discursive work is expended on ensuring that alternative medicine is considered inferior, amateurish and falling within the sphere of charlatans, thus maintaining for medical science the authority of the 'true' and the 'scientific'. Thus, discourses do not exist in a vacuum but are in constant conflict with other discourses and other social practices which inform them over questions of truth and authority. As Foucault puts it: 'I want to try to discover how this choice of truth, inside which we are caught but which we ceaselessly renew, was made – but also how it was repeated, renewed and displaced' (Foucault, 1981: 70). Thus, Foucault is not interested in which discourse is a true or accurate representation of the 'real', in this case whether alternative therapies work more effectively than conventional medicine; rather he is concerned with the mechanics whereby one becomes produced as the dominant discourse, which is supported by institutional funding, by the provision of buildings and staff by the state, and by the respect of the population as a whole, whereas the other is treated with suspicion and is housed both metaphorically and literally at the margins of society.

Power is therefore a key element in discussions of discourse. Foucault has been instrumental in the rethinking of models of power; rather than simply assuming, as many liberal humanists have, that power is a possession (so that someone takes or seizes power from someone else) or that power is a violation of someone's rights (for example, the idea that power is simply preventing someone from doing what they want to do) or, as Marxist theorists have, that power relations are determined by economic relations, Foucault has attempted to come to terms with the complexity of the range of practices which can be summed up under the term power. He is very critical of what he terms the 'repressive hypothesis' that power is simply about preventing someone from carrying out their wishes and limiting people's freedom. John Frow puts it this way:

> If power is no longer thought simply as a negative and repressive force but as the condition of production of all speech, and if power is conceived as polar rather than monolithic, as an asymmetrical dispersion, then all utterances will be potentially splintered, formally open to contradictory uses.
>
> (Frow, 1985: 206)

This sums up the sense of Foucault's analysis of power, that is, that power is dispersed throughout social relations, that it produces possible forms of behaviour as well as restricting behaviour. This productive model of power is something many theorists have found useful, particularly when looking at ways of thinking about discourse. In thinking about the sexuality of children, in *The History of Sexuality*, Volume I, Foucault gives an example of the way in which power relations produce forms of subjectivity and behaviour rather than simply repressing them. Speaking particularly about views of children's masturbation and sexuality within the Victorian period, he states:

> It would be less than exact to say that the pedagogical institution has imposed a ponderous silence on the sex of children and adolescents. On the contrary, since the eighteenth century it has multiplied the forms of discourse on the subject; it has established various points of implantation for sex; it has coded contents and qualified speakers. Speaking about children's sex, inducing educators, physicians, administrators, and parents to speak of it, or speaking to them about it, causing children themselves to talk about it, and enclosing them in a web of discourses which sometimes address them, sometimes speak about them, or impose canonical bits of knowledge on them, or use them as a basis for constructing a science that is beyond their grasp – all this together enables us to link an intensification of the interventions of power to a multiplication of discourse.
>
> (Foucault, 1978: 32)

Thus, far from institutional pressures repressing children's sexuality, in fact, as Foucault goes on to discuss, this discursive work created the forms within which that sexuality could appear:

> Educators and doctors combatted children's onanism [male masturbation] like an epidemic that needed to be eradicated. What this actually entailed, throughout this whole secular campaign that mobilized the adult world around the sex of children, was using these tenuous pleasures as a prop, constituting them as secrets (that is, forcing them into hiding so as to make possible their discovery), tracing them back to their source . . . wherever there was a chance they might appear, devices of surveillance were installed; traps were laid for compelling admissions; inexhaustible and corrective discourses were imposed; parents and teachers were alerted, and left with the suspicion that all children were guilty.
>
> (ibid.: 42)

As Foucault goes on to argue, this vigilance around the question of male children's masturbation, rather than eradicating the practice, was one of the factors which led to an increasing sexualisation of childhood in the Victorian period.

Foucault argues for the imbrication of power with knowledge, so that all of the knowledge we have is the result or the effect of power struggles. To give an example, what is studied in schools and universities is the result of struggles over whose version of events is sanctioned. Knowledge is often the product of the subjugation of objects, or perhaps it can be seen as the process through which subjects are constituted as subjugated; for example, when consulting a university library catalogue, if you search under the term 'women', you will find a vast selection of books and articles discussing the oppression of women, the psychology of women, the physical ailments that women suffer from, and so on. If you search under the term 'men' you will not find the same wealth of information. (In Chapter 4 I will analyse closely the relation between feminist theory and discourse theory.) Similarly, if you consult the catalogue again and look up 'India' or 'Africa', you will find that in the nineteenth century the production of knowledge about these countries by British writers coincided with the period when there was the greatest degree of colonial involvement. (I will also go on to consider this issue in Chapter 5 on colonial and post-colonial discourse theory.) Foucault has described this connection between the production of knowledge and power relations as 'power/knowledge' (Foucault, 1980a). Most theorists of power have seen individuals as oppressed by power relations, but Foucault sees them as the effects or instances of power relations:

> The individual is not to be conceived of as a sort of elementary nucleus . . . on which power comes to fasten. . . . In fact, it is already one of the prime effects of power that certain bodies, certain gestures, certain discourses, certain desires, come to be identified and constituted as individuals.
>
> (ibid.: 98)

Here the individual is seen as an effect of power and not that which is acted upon by power.

LITERATURE AS A DISCOURSE

Although not all of the readers of this book will be students of literary or cultural studies, these are perhaps the areas in which Foucault's work has been most influential. It may therefore be asked why Foucault's notion of discourse is important for literary and cultural studies, because although Foucault did analyse some literature, mainly in the form of reviews, literature was certainly not his primary concern, and in his theoretical work he does not produce textual analyses as such. In some ways, discourse as a term is most important for the questions it allows us to ask about literature and textuality in general. Literature has been variously designated by different theorists as a privileged site of critique or as an arbitrary set of conventions which we learn to read as literary, whereas as Macdonnell states:

> The methods and concepts of recent study of discourse make possible an analysis of the discourses, in their relation to institutional practices, through which a division of texts has been marked out and 'literature' has been constituted as the object of a certain enshrinement.

(Macdonnell, 1986: 7)

The study of discourse does not differentiate between those texts which are designated as literary and those which are designated as non-literary, although discourse theorists are keenly aware of the institutionalised differences that exist between the two sets of texts. History texts are privileged in their relation to truth, for example; autobiographical writings are privileged in terms of their supposed authenticity in relation to an authorial voice; and literary texts have a complex relation to both truth and value, on the one hand being seen as providing a 'truth' about the human condition, and yet doing so within a fictional and therefore 'untrue' form. However, for the discussion of the construction, say, of discourses of femininity and masculinity, it is possible to discuss literary texts alongside other texts, such as works of history and autobiography, and even more ephemeral texts, such as cookery books, advice manuals and so on, in order to reveal the similarities these texts display across generic boundaries. Discourse is therefore useful in that it can allow us to analyse similarities across a range of texts as the products of a particular set of power/ knowledge relations.

Foucault can be seen as having held particularly conservative ideas about literature; for example, in arguing for it to be considered as a privileged zone where language is used in non-referential ways. However, in most instances where Foucault is discussing literature he is describing avant-garde writing, and not literature in general. For example, he states:

> there has of course existed in the Western world, since Dante, since Homer, a form of language that we now call 'literature'. But the word [literature] is of recent date, as is also, in our culture, the isolation of a particular language whose peculiar mode of being is 'literary'. . . . Literature is the contestation of philology . . . it leads language back from grammar to the naked power of speech, and there it encounters the untamed, imperious being of words.
>
> (Foucault, 1970: 299–300)

Here Foucault seems to be characterising literature as a particular type of self-reflexive writing, since he goes on to describe literature as

> a silent, cautious deposition of the word upon the whiteness of a piece of paper, where it can possess neither sound nor interlocutor, where it has nothing to say but itself, nothing to do but shine in the brightness of its being.
>
> (ibid.: 300)

However, he also analyses the processes of exclusion which operate around institutions such as literature, and the critical discourses which are necessary to support and keep literary texts in circulation. As I show in Chapter 3 on discursive structures, the constituents of discourse itself are less important than the range of practices which are necessary to support that discourse and to exclude other discourses from positions of authority.

Foucault's work has helped a number of theorists to consider the way that English literature as a discipline works. Foucault himself states:

> literary criticism and literary history in the eighteenth and nineteenth centuries constituted the person of the author, and the figure of the oeuvre, using, modifying and displacing the procedures of religious exegesis, biblical criticism, hagiography, historical or legendary 'lives', autobiography or memoirs.
>
> (Foucault, 1981: 71)

This move to analyse the support given to literature as a discourse and as an institution, and the cannibalising of previous discourses by literary critics, has been an important move away from text-immanent analyses of literature, where, for example, the Renaissance or the eighteenth century are seen as 'natural' self-contained categories not invented by scholars. As Brian Doyle, Chris Baldick and Terry Eagleton have shown, although the study of literature feels familiar and 'normal', it became institutionalised at a crucial moment in English cultural history when religious faith was declining and when there was pressure to open up areas of study for those who had been previously excluded from formal education (i.e., women and the working classes) (Doyle, 1982; Baldick, 1983; Eagleton, 1983). Indeed, the study of literature was undertaken using very much the same discursive structures as those previously used for the study of religion, with the construction of canons (itself a religious categorisation of texts) and the focus on morality and values. As Brian Doyle has noted 'the teaching of a "national" language and literature operates as a key feature in reproducing the cultural relations within what is usually called "our" society' (Doyle, 1982: 17).

It should also be stated that, given a Foucauldian frame of reference, literature, as well as being the means whereby a sense of a national culture is established, is also the means whereby those norms of a shared culture can be contested. This contestation can be seen with the growth of women's studies courses and the inclusion of more women's writing on the mainstream literature syllabus, together with Black writing and writing in English. But, as Doyle states:

> It needs to be noted immediately that "the English language and literature" as a field of semantic and practical activity did not simply arrive on the scene from nowhere, full and complete. It had to be worked for, constructed, forged out of struggles between differing lived meanings and cultural forms.
>
> (ibid.: 19)

In the same way that the sense of a national culture or canon had to be worked for, the contestation of the form of that national culture is also something which has involved struggle.

This is why Foucault's archaeological analysis of discourse is important; he is not interested in simply analysing the discourses which are circulating in our society at present, what he wants us to see is the arbitrariness of this range of discourses, the strangeness of those discourses, in spite of their familiarity. He also wants to chart the development of certain discursive practices, so that we can see that, rather than being permanent, as their familiarity would suggest, discourses are constantly changing and their origins can be traced to certain key shifts in history. Although Foucault's notion of historiography has been criticised (Hacking, 1986; Taylor, 1986; Walzer, 1986), it is important to stress the uniqueness of Foucault's work in attempting to chart the changes in discursive structures over time. For Foucault, a discourse is not a set of utterances which is stable over time; he tries to work against the notions of progress and development which dominate many liberal ways of thinking. Instead of viewing history, for example, as a simple progression towards greater civilisation or, as Marxists have done, as a series of class conflicts which lead to greater equality, Foucault has argued that history is discontinuous; there is not a seamless narrative which we can decipher underlying history, nor is there any continuity at all. He argues for seeing history as discontinuous, as shifting and lurching in ways which are not entirely within human grasp, and not entirely within our control. He said in an interview:

> My problem has not at all been to say: there it is, long live discontinuity . . . but to pose the question: how can it be that there are at certain moments and in certain orders of knowledge these sudden take-offs, these hastenings of evolution, these transformations which do not correspond to the calm and continuist image that is ordinarily accepted.
>
> (Foucault, 1979e: 31)

Foucault is therefore concerned with charting these moments of discontinuity when discursive structures undergo radical change.

In this book, I aim to detail the use Foucault himself made of the term discourse and, in Chapter 2, to contrast its use with that of the term ideology. Since Marxist thinking was such a crucial reactive force in the development of the notion of discourse for Foucault, it is important to chart the history of that difference of meaning and emphasis. In Chapter 3 I analyse the structures that go to make up the building blocks of discourse. I then go on, in Chapters 4 and 5, to discuss the modifications that have been made to the definition of discourse by feminist theorists and colonial and post-colonial discourse theorists. These chapters serve also as examples of the way that the term discourse can be useful in textual analysis. In Chapter 6, I examine some of the work in linguistics which focuses on the term discourse, covering both the earlier discourse analysts and the more Foucauldian-influenced critical linguists and social psychologists. This book will thus circle around the meanings associated with the term discourse and around the complex matrix of issues concerning knowledge, truth and power, in order to define the parameters of its usage. The purpose of this circling around will not be to privilege one particular set of meanings which the term has accrued, nor to suggest that one set of interpretations of the term are 'true' or more adequate than others. Nor am I attempting to fossilise one particular set of meanings for the term. Rather, I am concerned throughout this book to focus on the limitations and theoretical difficulties which beset the term and perhaps to suggest ways in which these difficulties might be used as stepping-off points for further theoretical investigation.

NOTE

1   Michel Foucault had numerous rather heated debates about the meaning of the word 'statement'. In some of these discussions it was asserted that the statement was the same as the speech act, as

developed by John Austin and John Searle. See Dreyfus and Rabinow (1982: 44–49) for a fuller discussion, and also the section in Chapter 3 on the statement (pp. 60–62).

2

DISCOURSE AND IDEOLOGY

For all cultural and critical theorists there has been intense theoretical difficulty in deciding whether to draw on work which is based around the notion of ideology or work which refers to discourse. These problems have to do with political orientation, which, in the pessimistic political climate of the 1990s, has meant that many theorists have found themselves more comfortable dealing with notions of discourse than aligning themselves with Marxist-inflected theories through the use of the term ideology. This is not to suggest that discourse is necessarily an apolitical term, or that it signals a lack of political commitment, since, as I argue in Chapters 4 and 5, it is possible to conduct a politically informed analysis based on the use of discourse theory, but this political commitment is in no way as straightforwardly formulated as it is when using the term ideology. Thus, many theorists, after the collapse of the Soviet Union and the seeming world-wide collapse of communism as a viable political system, wanted to develop an intellectual practice concerned to analyse the determinants of thinking and behaviour in a more complex way than is possible when using terms like ideology. For many working with a vulgar Marxist model, ideology implied a simplistic and negative process whereby individuals were duped into using conceptual systems which were not in their own interests. Discourse, because of its lack of alliance to a clear political agenda, offered a way of thinking about hegemony – people's compliance in their own oppression – without assuming that individuals are necessarily simply passive victims of systems of thought. For those who work within discourse theory, the model of political activity and the perceived outcomes of that activity are very different from those developed within schools of thought informed by notions of ideology. Whereas Marxist views of history and progress tend to lead to fairly clear-cut Utopian views of what is to be achieved (a revolution, a remodelling of the economy, an alleviation of oppression of the working class, a widespread critique of consumerism and capitalism), models of action formulated using discourse tend to formulate rather messy, complex visions of the future. This is because, as I hope to show in this chapter, within discourse theory, questions of agency are less clear and, as a consequence, questions of how much control one has over what happens as a result of one's own actions are very much to the fore. Therefore, whilst political action can be accounted for theoretically within discourse theory, at the same time it is clear that one's actions may have several effects which do not match one's intentions. For example, you might intend simply to prevent the live export of veal calves through demonstrating outside British ports; this might in fact be one of the outcomes of your presence in the demonstration. However, another outcome might also be that you are photographed by the police and a file is opened on you as a potential agitator. Exporters might decide to employ security guards and also to use air freight rather than sea transport. The government might decide to bring in new legislation aimed at restricting the number of people allowed to demonstrate at any one time. Whereas a Marxist analysis of collective actions such as demonstrations would only be concerned with the immediate effects in relation to live animal export (the effect that had been intended), discourse theory would be as interested in the other outcomes, which it would see as similarly entailed by such action.

Foucault was working at a time when academic allegiance to Marxism in France was being questioned and when there was a great deal of debate about the possibility of forging a new type of political theorising drawing on Marxist thought but not involving the type of doctrinaire thinking which often accompanied some Marxist theory in France at the time. Foucault at various times openly acknowledged his debt to Marxist thought and at other times also sought clearly to distinguish and distance his work from Marxist thinking. What is clear is that Marxism and notions of ideology were crucial for him in the development of the notion of discourse.

The political events of May 1968 in Paris seemed to galvanise many academics, including Foucault, who were searching for a way of acting and of questioning liberal humanist and conservative orthodoxies. The student unrest and the subsequent wider unrest involving workers and other groups drew many academics into open political activity, campaigning and demonstrating alongside and for the rights of workers, homosexuals, prisoners and others (Macey, 1993). During the 1970s Foucault was actively involved in a number of campaigns and was often called upon to act as a figurehead for certain actions. For example, in 1971 Foucault became involved with a group of prisoners who were demanding rights and political status under a particularly harsh prison regime; with them Foucault set up the Groupe d'Information sur les Prisonniers (GIP), which aimed to give voice to prisoners and allow them access to the debates which were taking place in the public sphere about the conditions in prisons. He also became involved in the struggle for Algerian independence and for a wide range of political movements which gained greatly from the very visible presence of a well-known public figure. Thus, although discourse theory is often characterised as apolitical, Foucault's work can best be seen as a debate with Marxism about what is possible as a form of political action and, particularly, his work should be seen as an intense debate about the role of the intellectual in political struggle.

Much of Foucault's work on discourse has been an open discussion and dialogue with the term ideology, and in some sense the term discourse has been defined in dialogue with and in reaction to the definition of ideology. There are a number of differences between the terms discourse and ideology which I would like to examine in some detail. Firstly, let us consider what Foucault himself has to say on this:

> The notion of ideology appears to me to be difficult to use for three reasons. The first is that, whether one wants it to be or not, it is always in virtual opposition to something like the truth. . . . The second inconvenience is that it refers, necessarily I believe, to something like a subject. Thirdly, ideology is in a secondary position in relation to something which must function as the infra-structure or economic or material determinant for it.
>
> (Foucault, 1979e: 36)

Let us consider these differences which Foucault has found between ideology and discourse in some detail. Firstly, let us take the opposition of ideology to a position of truth or critique which is located outside ideology.

IDEOLOGY AND TRUTH

The theorising of ideology, especially the work of Louis Althusser, is based on the notion that the position from which the theorist speaks is one of scientific critique (see Althusser, 1984; Eagleton, 1991). Thus, ideology is often characterised as false consciousness or an imagined representation of the real conditions of existence; the position from which this falseness is apprehended is that of critique and stands outside ideology. Foucault, however, does not hold that his own position is completely outside the ideas and practices which he is analysing. For some, this has meant that Foucault's own theoretical position is fundamentally undermined, since it seems to suggest that, within a discourse theory view, all statements – whether theoretical or not – have the same status and validity; that is, any act of critique is determined and formed by the power relation of which it is a part. It seems also to suggest that all statements are similarly determined by institutional pressures. This makes it difficult to distinguish between statements and acts which oppose oppression and those which are complicit with that oppression. However, this seeming relativism does not invalidate Foucault's own critical position and in fact is completely in line with his own theoretical statements on truth. Foucault is not claiming to speak from a position of 'truth' – he is aware of the fact that he himself as a subject can only speak within the limits imposed upon him by the discursive frameworks circulating at the time. That does not mean that it is not possible to be critical, but there are limits to what can be thought and, particularly, there are limits on what can be classified as 'knowable'. The notion within ideology of false consciousness assumes that there is a consciousness which is not false (the position of critique); for Foucault, all knowledge is determined by a combination of social, institutional and discursive pressures, and theoretical knowledge is no exception. Some of this knowledge will challenge dominant discourses and some will be complicit with them.

THE SUBJECT

Foucault was concerned to write about the history of ideas without referring to the sovereign subject – the individual. He tried to move away from the notion of the Cartesian subject, the subject whose existence depends on its ability to see itself as unique and as self-contained, distinct from others, because it can think and reason. By refusing to refer to the subject as a unitary being, Foucault is very much part of post-structuralist thinking, which questioned the very fundamental bases of liberal humanist ideology, rooted as it is in the notion of the individual self with agency and control over itself. Post-structuralist psychoanalytic theory questioned the unity of the subject, finding it more useful to analyse the subject-in-process or the subject-in-crisis, that is, the disintegration of the notion of the unified subject (Moi, 1986; Vice, 1996). Psychoanalysts describe the wide range of subject positions which individuals inhabit precariously, sometimes wilfully adopting particular subject roles and sometimes finding themselves being cast into certain roles because of their past developmental history or because of the actions of others. This focus on a range of shifting and precarious subject positions means that the subject is no longer seen to be in control. However, Foucault went further than these models of the self developed within psychoanalysis (and adopted by Marxist theorists such as Althusser), since he tried to formulate a way of examining historical processes without relying on the notion of the subject. Foucault found it necessary to start his analyses elsewhere and shift the centre of attention away from the subject entirely. Perhaps this is where his work is most controversial, since he is concerned to see the subject as simply an effect of power and in a sense to chart the death of the subject. Rather than seeing the subject or even the subject-in-crisis as an element whose existence and features could be charted, Foucault chose rather to ignore the subject in itself, and concentrate on the processes which he considered to be important in the constitution of our very notion of subjectivity. Particularly in *The Archaeology of Knowledge* (1972) and *The History of Sexuality*, Volume I (1978), he sees his task as charting the changes in the production and circulation of knowledge which led to the notion of subjectivity becoming of such fundamental importance for Western societies since the eighteenth century, and this focus constitutes for him a change in historical method:

One had to dispense with the constituent subject, to get rid of the subject itself, that's to say, to arrive at an analysis which can account for the constitution of the subject within a historical framework. And this is what I would call genealogy, that is, a form of history which can account for the constitution of knowledges, discourses, domains of objects, etc., without having to make reference to a subject which is either transcendental in relation to the field of events or runs in its empty sameness throughout the course of history.

(Foucault, 1980a: 59)

Later in his work, he did return to the question of the subject, not to write the subject into history as such but to situate the historical changes and constitution of the concept of the sexed subject (Foucault, 1985). This is perhaps where discourse theory seems to be disengaged from a concern with individuals or groups of people, since, for example, Foucault sees the invention of the homosexual as a type of person, in the eighteenth and nineteenth centuries, to have been the result of a number of changes within Western knowledge about the nature of sexuality, rather than a simple expression of the sexual preference of an individual self. An ideological analysis may downplay the importance of the subject because of its concern with groups or classes of individuals, and because of its interest in the construction of individual subjectivity through the actions of institutions such as the state. However, an ideological analysis still, in the last instance, retains the notion of the individual subject who is capable of resisting ideological pressures and controlling his or her actions. Discourse theory has far more difficulty in locating, describing and even accounting for this individual subject who resists power.

DETERMINANTS OF DISCOURSE

Foucault did not believe that there was a simple relationship between economic and social structures and discourses. He did not believe, as some Marxists do, that the economic base determines what can be said and thought at a particular time; instead, he saw the relation between economics, social structures and discourses as being a complex interaction with none of the terms of the equation being dominant. Whilst he was very aware of the importance of state control and power relations based on economic imbalance, he did not see economic relations as primary, but as one type of power relation within a range of power relations. Foucault was also concerned to show that power relations were not, as many Marxist theorists had tried to show, coterminous with economic relations. He tried to move the analysis of power relations within capitalism away from assuming that certain structures of power and capitalism are the same, as Patton comments:

> It is not, perhaps, capitalist production which is autocratic and hierarchised, but disciplinary production which is capitalist. We know after all that disciplinary organisation of the workforce persists even when production is no longer strictly speaking capitalist.
>
> (Patton, 1979: 124)

This is a matter of interest, particularly after the collapse of the Eastern bloc, since it is clear that the seeming disintegration of the socialist apparatus has in fact brought about few major changes in the exploitative relations of production in Eastern Europe. It may be that there are more forces at work in the organisation of industrial labour within this context than a simple matter of communist ideology.

I would like now to consider some further differences between conceptions of ideology and Foucault's notion of discourse, for example, the relation of discourse and ideology to notions of power. As Foucault states: 'If power was never anything but repressive, if it never did anything but say no, do you really believe that we should manage to obey it?' (Foucault, 1979e: 36). Marxist thought in particular seems to characterise power within what Foucault termed the 'repressive hypothesis', that is, it sees power as simply a negative infringement on someone else's rights; here, power is taken or seized from others, and it is viewed as something which one can possess or hold at another's expense. Foucault tries to move the conception of power away from this negative model towards a framework which stresses its productive nature, that it produces as well as represses. The example Foucault gives is contained within *The History of Sexuality*, Volume I, where he discusses the repression of children's sexuality in the nineteenth century. He argues that attempts to regulate (male) children's masturbation in fact undoubtedly produced the very sexuality that they were trying to eradicate. Parents' interventions actually produced different types of pleasures because of the perceived need for the child to hide such sexual practices, and this in a sense structured the child's sexuality. This sense of surveillance of children and the treating of masturbation as an epidemic that needed to be eradicated entailed a certain vigilance on both the parents' and the child's part, and therefore a certain awareness and foregrounding of sexuality:

> Wherever there was a chance they [traces of sexual behaviour] might appear, devices of surveillance were installed; traps were laid for compelling admissions; inexhaustible and corrective discourses were imposed; parents and teachers were alerted, and left with the suspicion that all children were guilty, and with the fear of being themselves at fault if their suspicions were not sufficiently strong; they were kept in readiness in the face of this recurrent danger; their conduct was prescribed and their pedagogy recodified; an entire medico-sexual regime took hold of the family regime. The child's 'vice' was not so much an enemy as a support; it may have been designated as the evil to be eliminated, but the extraordinary effort that went into the task was bound to fail which leads one to suspect that what

was demanded of it was to persevere, to proliferate to the limits of the visible and the invisible, rather than to disappear for good.

(Foucault, 1979a)

Thus, counter-intuitively, the seeming repression of male children's sexuality served only to produce a particular type of pleasurable sexual practice within the confines of secrecy and guilt.[1] In *The History of Sexuality*, Foucault also details the way that homosexuality was produced as a sexual practice and as a type of personality in the very process whereby sexologists attempted to describe homosexual acts as deviant and perverted. Thus, the notion that repression of acts by those in power simply results in the erasing of those acts is a simplistic model of actions and power relations; it is clear from Foucault's work that forms of subjectivity are produced in negotiation with existing power relations.

Whilst Marxist theorists tend to stress the importance of the State in the maintenance of power relations and in the distribution of access to the means of the mode of production, Foucault is at great pains to develop a different model of power which does not locate power as a possession within the hands of a monolithic State. Although Marxists such as Louis Althusser complicate the notion of the State by trying to formulate a model of State power which has a dispersion of agents of the State throughout society, in the final analysis, the State is still the supreme determinant and source of power relations (Althusser, 1984). Instead of this institutional focus, Foucault says: 'I don't want to say that the State isn't important; what I want to say is that relations of power . . . necessarily extend beyond the limits of the State' (Foucault, 1979e: 38). This notion of moving views of power away from a fixation on the State and hence on a top-down model of power is important in the sense that it enables us to see power as a relation rather than a simple imposition. This relation involves more possible role positions than simply that of master–slave presupposed in the

State power model; it also involves an analysis of the degrees of power involved in the relation rather than an assumption that in any power relation there is simply a powerful participant and a powerless one.

Foucault argues strongly against the notion of the repressive hypothesis, as shown above, because for him it is clear that power circulates through a society rather than being owned by one group. Power is not so easily contained. Power is more a form of action or relation between people which is negotiated in each interaction and is never fixed and stable. Whilst Foucault would not minimise the importance of the power of the State, he would suggest that power operates around and through the networks which are generated around the institutions of the State; in some senses power has always been more thoroughly dispersed through-out society than had been realised. For example, a Marxist analysis of prisons would discuss the oppression and harsh treatment of the inmates, focusing on the curtailment of rights and liberty, and perhaps would concentrate on the ways that prisoners resist the penal regime. A discourse theory analysis would be more concerned with the structures through which that power relation is manifested in the prison. For example, Foucault has described the architectural organisation of space in the prison so that each prisoner has the sense that s/he is under surveillance even when that is not in fact the case (Foucault, 1979a). He has also gone on to describe the process whereby those disciplinary structures have informed the way that other power relations are lived out in the wider contexts of schools, churches and military institutions, so that individuals learn to discipline themselves or learn self-discipline through this notion that they are potentially under surveillance.

Foucault is also more concerned with the ways in which people negotiate power relations, rather than assuming that the powerful person in a institutionalised relation is in fact all-powerful. For example, in work I have undertaken on the way that secretaries speak to their bosses, I have found that there is not a clear-cut distinction to be made between powerful talk, on the one hand, and powerless talk on the other. Particularly through their verbal dexterity and use of language, those who are not in economically powerful positions, may nevertheless manage to negotiate for themselves fairly powerful positions in the hierarchy (Mills, 1992a, 1996d). Furthermore, those who are in powerful positions may have to be careful how they negotiate the enactment of their power, and may have to temper the types of direct commands that they give. For example, a stereotypical view of a power relation between a secretary and a boss would produce an interaction such as the following:

> Boss: I want this letter typed up by the afternoon post.
> Secretary: Yes, certainly.

Here, the boss manifests in his utterance the fact that he is in an economically and institutionally sanctioned privileged position in relation to the secretary and is thus able to issue her with direct commands (or, in this case, statements of his needs that she will interpret as commands). The secretary will also signal to the boss her acknowledgement of her inferior position by her compliance to his command.[2] However, in most interactions between bosses and secretaries that I have analysed, this type of powerful/powerless verbal structure rarely occurs. What is far more common is for the boss to display deference and tentativeness to the secretary (seemingly classic signs of powerlessness) and for the secretary to be very resistant to complying with the requests made by the boss (seemingly classic signs of a powerful position). Here is an example from one of the interactions which I recorded:

> Boss: I wonder . . . if . . . er . . . could you possibly . . .
> you know, this report thing here . . . could that be
> sort of sent out // this afternoon
> Secretary: // Well. I've got a lot of work on

　　　　　　// but I suppose. . .

Boss:　　　// I'd really appreciate it thanks

(Mills, 1996d); . . . indicates pause, // indicates simultaneous speech)

Here the boss displays all of the signs of powerlessness – hesitating, hedging (using 'sort of', 'report thing' rather than 'report', 'I wonder if you could possibly' rather than a bare command) – and he even avoids stating explicitly his command: he only asks if the report could be sent out and not if his secretary could make the necessary revisions before sending it out. The secretary does not answer in the affirmative; instead, she tells the boss about how busy she is, implicitly stating that she cannot do the work. However, once she says 'but', the boss realises that she will do the work and thanks her. Even here, the secretary does not say that she will willingly do the work, for she only says 'I suppose [I will do the work]'. It is clear that secretaries cannot refuse to undertake tasks which their bosses have asked them to do, but they can certainly make it evident to their bosses that each request that they make will have to be couched in polite, deferent language which acknowledges the effort the task will entail. This is not to suggest that in all interactions between bosses and secretaries the secretaries in fact hold the position of power; rather, it suggests ways in which people who have been assigned a fairly powerless position within a hierarchy negotiate with that position and accrue power to themselves through their use of seemingly powerful styles of language (see also Holmes, 1995).

Within the theorising of ideology, whilst great stress is laid on the overthrow of repressive power relations, it is difficult at a theoretical level to account for the fact that revolutions do in fact take place. The emphasis within Marxist theory is on the nature of the oppressive power relations and, whilst the notion of the revolutionary subject is central to this process because of the characterisation of power as oppressive, it is sometimes hard to understand how subjects can develop a revolutionary consciousness, how they can resist oppression. Foucault argues that resistance is already contained within the notion of power: 'Where there is power there is resistance', as he puts it. This is a very attractive concept, since for Foucault no power relation is simply one of total domination. Entailed within that relation is the force which may challenge or overthrow it. For many feminist theorists this notion of resistance being always present within power relations has been particularly useful and has helped move theory away from a concern with oppressor–victim models of dominance, which had been prevalent in early feminist thinking. It also helped many theorists within post-colonial theorising, since it consolidated concerns around the issue of analysing resistance to colonial rule rather than simply charting the workings of colonial power (see Guha and Spivak, 1988). However, as Macdonnell puts it: 'If power is always already there, if every power situation is immanent in itself, why should there ever be resistance? From where would resistance come and how would it even be possible?' (Macdonnell, 1986: 122) This is a major criticism, and it is one which I will be considering in more detail in the chapters on feminism and colonial discourse theory. For the moment, it is important to stress that Foucault's conception of power enables us to see the complexities of power – that power is not simply an imposition. In order to deal with questions of agency (which is crucial to both feminist and post-colonial theory) however, it is necessary to modify Foucault's work.

LANGUAGE, DISCOURSE AND IDEOLOGY

Foucault's conceptualisation of power forces us to re-evaluate the role of language/discourse/texts in the process of the constitution of subjects within a hierarchy of relations. Some Marxist theorists have tended to view language as simply a vehicle whereby people are forced to believe ideas which are not true or in their interests but, within discourse theory, language is the site where those struggles are acted out; as Foucault states: 'as history constantly teaches us, discourse is not simply that which translates struggles or systems of domination, but is the thing for which and by which there is struggle' (Foucault, 1981: 52–3). A good example of the contrast between theorists who base their work around notions of ideology and those who draw on discourse theory would be the debates over political correctness/sexism (for overviews see Dunant, 1994; Sunderland, 1994; Mills, 1995a). For both groups of theorists, sexism consists of those statements and underlying beliefs which make unnecessary and discriminatory distinctions between people on the grounds of gender (Vetterling-Braggin, 1981). For example, referring to Suzanne Charlton as a 'weather-girl' and Michael Fish as a 'weatherman' would be considered to be sexist, since Fish is assigned adult status and Charlton is given the term normally assigned to a child; this is a common strategy within sexism whereby women are consigned to a less powerful position, even when they are in fact in an equally powerful position to men. Similarly, stating that 'women make terrible drivers' would be considered to be sexist, because it assumes that all women behave in a similar way and makes it appear that this is part of the nature of being female. Thus, the statement is sexist because it is a globalising assertion which makes a connection between elements which have no connection with the condition of being female (see Mills, 1995a for a fuller discussion).

Both ideological critics and discourse theorists would agree on which statements count as sexist. However, within an ideological view, sexism would be seen as a form of false consciousness, a way that subjects were, in Althusserian terms, interpellated, that is, called upon to recognise themselves as certain types of gendered subjects (Spender, 1980; Althusser, 1984). By accepting sexism within language, subjects are called upon to recognise themselves as taking up a position within a hierarchised system of gendered differentiation; thus, sexism forces subjects into an acceptance of the *status quo* and of prevalent views of women as inferior and sexually available to men, with men as superior, in control, and so on. Dale Spender's ideological analysis of sexism would see sexism as an indicator of men's wider control over women as a group and an index of the systematic nature of patriarchy (Spender, 1980). However, whilst this is a useful first stage in analysing sexism, one which enables us to recognise the process whereby sexism comes to feel 'natural' or dominant within a culture, it does not allow us any real sense of how it would be possible to intervene and change that process. In Spender's view, women are seen as victims of male oppression and are homogenised as a group, unable to intervene in the process whereby they are oppressed.

A discourse theory perspective enables us to question whether sexism is ever simply a matter of the imposition of a set of beliefs on a group of subjects. The debate around sexism has been a struggle to change words, a struggle over language, at the same time as it has been a struggle over legitimacy and about who has the right to define the usage of language, as well as who has the right to decide what is studied in schools and universities. Although much of the debate has been muddied by arguments about freedom of speech and curtailment of freedoms, the struggle itself has highlighted the conflicts and tensions which exist in educational institutions particularly, over the entry of women and ethnic minorities to positions of power. Perhaps, indeed, one of the major effects of campaigns over sexist language within educational institutions has been less a change of language (although it is clear that this has taken place), but rather a fundamental exposing of sexist and racist structures. Thus, such campaigns have led to a position where it is not possible to sit on the fence; questions of language usage have led to wider political actions. As Foucault states:

> Discourses are not once and for all subservient to power or raised up against it, any more than silences are. We must make allowances for the complex and unstable process whereby

discourse can be both an instrument and an effect of power, but also a hindrance, a stumbling block, a point of resistance and a starting point for an opposing strategy. Discourse transmits and produces power; it reinforces it, but also undermines it and exposes it, renders it fragile and makes it possible to thwart it.

(Foucault, 1978: 100–1)

Thus, whilst within an ideological view sexism is an oppressive strategy employed by men to bolster their own power, within a discourse theory model, sexism *is* the site of contestation; it is both the arena where some males are sanctioned in their attempts to negotiate a powerful position for themselves in relation to women, but it is also the site where women can contest or collaborate with those moves. The fact that there have been strong efforts made by many conservatives to label struggles over sexist and racist language as mere political correctness – an implicitly negative term – and that feminists and anti-racists have attempted to resist that naming demonstrates the way that struggle over language is more than a simple imposition of a particular view on powerless people by people in power. As Deborah Cameron puts it:

the . . . movement for so-called 'politically correct' language does not threaten our freedom to speak as we choose, within the limits imposed by any form of social and public interaction. It threatens only our freedom to imagine that our linguistic choices are inconsequential, or to suppose that any one group of people has an inalienable right to prescribe them.

(Cameron, 1994: 33)

Thus, whilst the two positions both see sexism as being symptomatic of wider differentials in power, an ideological analysis, because of its view of power, is forced to characterise the female subject as powerless. A discourse theory view characterises subjects as engaging in their own constitution, acquiescing with or contesting the roles to which they are assigned.

There are many theorists who do not separate discourse and ideology so distinctly as terms as I have in this chapter, and many continue to use ideology as a term whilst situating themselves largely within a discourse theory framework (Fairclough, 1989; Hennessy, 1993). For some, discourse is the larger term within which there exist a range of different ideologies, whilst for others ideologies are made manifest through a variety of different discourses (Eagleton, 1991: 193–219). Eagleton tries to sum up this possible relation as follows:

> It may help to view ideology less as a particular *set* of discourses, than as a particular set of effects *within* discourses. Bourgeois ideology includes this particular discourse on property, that way of talking about the soul, this treatise on jurisprudence and the kind of utterances one overhears in pubs where the landlord wears a military tie. What is 'bourgeois' about this mixed bunch of idioms is less the *kind* of languages they are than the effects they produce: effects for example of closure whereby certain forms of signification are silently excluded, and certain signifiers 'fixed' in a commanding position.
>
> (ibid.: 194; italics in original)

Whilst Eagleton's view suggests ways in which the terms discourse and ideology may in fact work in tandem in analysis, for the purposes of this book it is quite useful to see these terms as distinct in order to map out the parameters of the usage of discourse. It is part of the history of the usage of the term discourse that it has been constituted in reaction to the meanings associated with the term ideology, and that struggle with the concept ideology is still a part of its current range of meanings.

NOTES

1   I should make it clear that, although Foucault discusses this type of repression in relation to children in general within the nineteenth century, it is clear that in fact he only has in mind male children. Female children were produced as asexual in a sense through this concentration on the repression of the seemingly more visible male child's masturbatory practices, a fact which Foucault does not consider.

2   For a stereotypical view of politeness and power relations, see Brown and Levinson (1978).

3

DISCURSIVE STRUCTURES

Structuralist thought focused largely on mapping out the rules governing the production of texts and systems of signification; theorists such as Roland Barthes and Michel Foucault were both interested not only in the structures which could be found in cultural artefacts, but also in the larger-scale structures which could be traced in discourse itself. One of the important assertions that Michel Foucault made in *The Archaeology of Knowledge* (1972) was that discourses are not simply groupings of utterances, grouped around a theme or an issue, nor are they simply sets of utterances which emanate from a particular institutional setting, but that discourses are highly regulated groupings of utterances or statements with internal rules which are specific to discourse itself. In this chapter, I discuss the constituents of discourse itself – the more abstract element within which particular discourses are produced. Discourse as a whole consists of regulated discourses. Discursive rules and structures do not originate from socio-economic or cultural factors as such, although they may be shaped to an extent by these factors; rather, they are a feature of discourse itself and are shaped by the internal mechanisms of discourse alone.

Both Barthes' and Foucault's later work moves away from this original premise, but it is still important to retain this notion of discourse being rule-governed and internally structured. Thus, the study of discourse is not simply the analysis of utterances and statements; it is also a concern with the structures and rules of discourse. These structures and rules are the focus of this chapter. Foucault termed this type of analysis of discursive structures 'archaeology'. For him archaeology:

> does not imply the search for a beginning; it does not relate to geological excavation. It designates the general theme of a description that questions the already-said at the level of its existence, of the enunciative function that operates within it, of the discursive formation, and the general archive system to which it belongs. Archaeology describes discourses as practices specified in the element of the archive.
>
> (Foucault, 1972: 131)

This description of archaeological analysis may seem particularly intractable at first sight; in fact, Foucault is simply trying to stress that the main reason for conducting an analysis of the structures of discourse is not to uncover the truth or the origin of a statement but rather to discover the support mechanisms which keep it in place. These support mechanisms are both intrinsic to discourse itself and also extra-discursive, in the sense that they are socio-cultural. Thus, in this quotation, Foucault is concerned to set statements in their discursive frameworks, that is, statements do not exist in isolation since there is a set of structures which makes those statements make sense and gives them their force.[1]

Before beginning a description of discursive structures, it is necessary to describe the relation between discourse and the real. The focus of *The Archaeology of Knowledge* is largely on the relation of texts and discourses to the real, and the construction of the real by discursive structures. There is a strong sense in which the real is characterised as a set of constructs formed through discourse. The real itself is never defined as such by Foucault, since for him we have access only to the discursive structures which determine our perceptions of the real. John Frow comments: 'The discursive is a socially constructed reality which constructs both the real and the symbolic and the distinction between them. It assigns structure to the real at the same time as it is a product and a moment of real structures' (Frow, 1985: 200). There has been a great deal of rather pointless debate about whether Foucault is in fact denying the existence of the real when he stresses the formative powers of discourse, and historians in particular have attacked him for denying the existence of historical events (see Taylor, 1986 for an overview). However, perhaps it is more useful to see Foucault's views on the relation between discourse and the real in the following terms, as set out by Laclau and Mouffe:

> The fact that every object is constituted as an object of discourse has nothing to do with whether there is a world external to thought, or with the realism/idealism opposition. An earthquake or the falling of a brick is an event that certainly exists, in the sense that it occurs here and now, independently of my will. But whether their specificity as objects is constructed in terms of 'natural phenomena' or 'expressions of the wrath of God', depends upon the structuring of a discursive field. What is denied is not that such objects exist externally to thought, but the rather different assertion that they could constitute themselves as objects outside any discursive condition of emergence.
>
> (Laclau and Mouffe, 1985: 108)

Thus, Foucault does not deny the existence of the real; on the contrary, he asserts that what we perceive to be significant and how we interpret objects and events and set them within systems of meaning is dependent on discursive structures. Those discursive structures are, for Foucault, what make objects and events appear to us to be real or material. This view of the materiality of discursive structures has, however, been questioned by many theorists, most notably by Terry Lovell, when she criticises this very determinist view: 'signs cannot be permitted to swallow up their referents in a never-ending chain of signification, in which one sign always points to another, and the circle is never broken by the intrusion of that to which the sign refers' (Lovell 1980: 16). However, whilst Foucault suggests that discourses structure our sense of reality, he does not see these systems as being abstract or enclosed. He is concerned with the way that discourses inform the extent to which we can think and act only within certain parameters at each historical conjuncture. Thus, although he sees the real as constructed through discursive pressures, he is also well aware of the effect of this 'reality' on thought and behaviour.

For Foucault, our perception of objects is formed within the limits of discursive constraints: discourse is characterised by a 'delimitation of a field of objects, the definition of a legitimate perspective for the agent of knowledge, and the fixing of norms for the elaboration of concepts or theories' (Foucault, 1977a: 199). Let us analyse the three assertions in this quotation in some detail. The first thing to notice is that, for Foucault, discourse causes a narrowing of one's field of vision, to exclude a wide range of phenomena from being considered as real or as worthy of attention, or as even existing; thus, delimiting a field is the first stage in establishing a set of discursive practices. Then, in order for a discourse or an object to be activated, to be called into existence, the knower has to establish a right for him/herself to speak. Thus, entry into discourse is seen to be inextricably linked to questions of authority and legitimacy. Finally, each act somehow maps out the possible uses which can be made of that statement, or future rules for its use (although of course that is not necessarily what happens to it). Each statement leads to others and, in a sense, it has to have embedded within it the parameters of the possible ways in which future statements can be made.

Discourse, for Foucault, constitutes objects for us. One of Foucault's most famous quotations about the constitution of objects is the following: 'We must not imagine that the world turns towards us a legible face which we would have only to decipher. The world is not the accomplice of our knowledge; there is no prediscursive providence which disposes the world in our favour' (Foucault, 1981: 67). That is, there is no intrinsic order to the world itself other than the ordering which we impose on it through our linguistic description of it. An example of this constitution of objects through discourse is the changes in the way the borderline between animals and plants has been drawn differently at different historical periods. In the nineteenth century, bacteria were placed within the category 'animal', whereas now they are located in a separate categorisation of their own. Several organisms have been switched from one category to another, for example, algae, diatoms and other micro-organisms. In fact, the categories 'plant' and 'animal' are constantly being redefined by which living things are placed within each categorisation – a *post-hoc* categorisation system which is discursive rather than one which is determined by the 'real' nature of plants and animals. Plants and animals, in fact, share many elements, but the fact that we separate them into two groupings means that we concentrate on the differences we perceive between these two categories rather than on their shared features. The fact that the boundary has shifted shows clearly that there is no natural ready-made boundary between animal and plant life, but that humans have thought it necessary to draw this boundary. It might be more useful for the difference between animals and plant to be thought of on a cline or continuum, but within current systems of thinking about this subject it is considered necessary to classify plant and animal life as separate. This could be related to the fact that we have moved away from the nineteenth-century polymath ability to undertake multi-disciplinary work; instead, at present, botany and zoology are seen as two separate sciences with separate departments in universities, and as separate disciplines with different methodologies and spheres of interest.

A further example of the way that discursive boundaries structure what we consider to be real categories might be Linnean typologies of plant categorisation. When nineteenth-century botanists travelled to foreign countries to investigate non-European plant species, they carried with them a categorisation system originally developed by Linneaus to categorise European plants. As Mary Louise Pratt has shown, this meant that the plants which were 'discovered' by Europeans within India and Africa were categorised within a European system of classification which aimed to be a global system (Pratt, 1992). The plants were extracted from the systems of classification which indigenous subjects had developed to describe their properties, uses and habitats, and they became part of a wider colonial project which aimed to demonstrate the 'civilising' force of colonialism. The plants were thus no longer seen in terms of their original classification system, which often related to their use in medicine, their food-value, their relation to other elements within an eco-system and their position within a cosmological and symbolic system, but rather they were seen out of context in terms of the similarity or dissimilarity of their morphology (plant structure) to European plant species. When the plant species were 'discovered' by Europeans, their names were changed from their indigenous names to classifications generated from the Linnean system (i.e., by analogy with previous Latin names) and often they were named after the European who had 'discovered' them. Thus, this global Eurocentric knowledge did not simply rename a few plant species, but annihilated indigenous knowledge and transformed the knowledge about plants in non-European countries into colonial knowledge (Mills, 1994b).

Discourse does not simply construct material objects, such as particular groups of plants; discourse also constructs certain events and sequences of events into narratives which are recognised by a particular culture as real or serious events. For example, within

Western cultures, miscarriage is considered to be simply a failed pregnancy, rather than the death of a baby. Therefore, there are no ritualised structures within which those who suffer miscarriages can deal with their loss. Through discourse, miscarriage is constructed as a failed event and not a real event in its own right. In a similar way, relationships which do not result in the couple living together or getting married are viewed by many people as not 'serious'. Thus, there is only one sanctioned narrative within the discourse of romantic love: there are many other pathways within which individuals work out their relations with other people, but this particular narrative sequence, which has as its end a formalised union of some sort, excludes certain types of relationships from being counted as real (Mills and White, forthcoming).

Foucault's position, which suggests that objects and ideas are created by humans and institutions and that it is this which constitutes reality for us, has been criticised because it seems to suggest that there is nothing which is non-discursive and outside discourse. But Foucault is not denying that there is a reality which pre-exists humans, nor is he denying the materiality of events and experience, as some of his critics have alleged; it is simply that the only way we have to apprehend reality is through discourse and discursive structures. In the process of apprehending, we categorise and interpret experience and events according to the structures available to us and, in the process of interpretation, we lend these structures a solidity and a normality which it is often difficult to think outside of. Foucault does not consider these structures to be simply the invention of institutions or powerful groups of people, as some Marxist thinkers have suggested in their formulating of the notion of ideology, nor does he propose that they are simply abstract and arbitrary. Rather, he considers that there is a combined force of institutional and cultural pressure, together with the intrinsic structure of discourse, which always exceeds the plans and desires of the institution or of those in power.

Roland Barthes' analysis of discursive structures, in *Fragments: A Lover's Discourse* (1990), is complementary to Foucault's work, in that he too is concerned to describe the structures within which individuals in love are at the mercy of the tropes, moods, emotions, gestures, tones of voice which the discourse of the lover lays out for them. Barthes considers all of these structured elements to constitute what he calls 'fragments', which make up the discourse as a whole. As he puts it:

> throughout any love life, figures occur to the lover without any order, for on each occasion they depend on an (internal or external?) accident . . . the amorous subject draws on a reservoir (the thesaurus?) of figures . . . the figures are non-syntagmatic, non-narrative.
>
> (Barthes, 1990: 6–7)

The questioning tone that Barthes adopts in this quotation is emblematic of his analysis of discursive structures as a whole – he wants to be able to describe the way that these figures determine the feelings and states which the lover experiences without concerning himself with explaining or discovering a source for these figures. Thus, he offers to the reader a list of alphabetically organised fragments which for him constitute the discourse of the lover; these figures are wide-ranging, from descriptions of states such as waiting, deception and absence, to analyses of the quality of language used by the lover. It is less an attempt to chart the 'grammar' of the lover's discourse than it is a testing of the limits of the personal within discourse. It is clear that he chose to analyse the lover's discourse since it is at one and the same time the experience which seems to most people to be the most deeply personal, and yet it is also that which is the most intensively discursively structured. Perhaps connected with this ambivalence is the fact that it is the experience which most tests one's powers of expression: Barthes suggests that it seems like 'the end of language' where in effect one repeats endlessly 'I love you because I love you' (ibid.:

21). Barthes' experiment with describing the discursive structures of love has wider implications for the analysis of discourse as a whole. The fragment as a constituent part of discourse is certainly a suggestive way of mapping out these structures.

However, in order to try to examine in more detail some of the constituents of discourse, I now turn to Foucault again, since his work is perhaps more 'grammatical' and in a sense more easily applicable to other contexts. I examine the structures which Foucault suggests are intrinsic to discourse, most notably the episteme, the statement, the discourse and the archive. Boundaries and limits are very important, in the sense of the function of these categories and structures, and I therefore go on to consider the ways in which perhaps the most important structure of discourse is less its constituent parts but rather the function of exclusion. Following on from this, I then consider the way that certain discourses are circulated and in effect kept in existence.

THE EPISTEME

The sense of the world of objects being constructed by institutions within social groups, particularly through language, has been a concern of a great many post-structuralist theorists and linguists. But perhaps Foucault is the only theorist who has seriously attempted to examine the change in these discursive systems over time and the changes that this subsequently causes to those cultures' views of reality. In *The Archaeology of Knowledge* (1972), Foucault attempts to chart these changes systematically so that he can map the discursive limits of an episteme, that is, the sets of discursive structures as a whole within which a culture thinks. Groups of discourses make up the structures of an episteme and, as Macdonnell states, an episteme 'may be understood as the ground of thought on which at a particular time some statements – and not others – will count as knowledge' (Macdonnell, 1986: 87). These groups of discursive units do not constitute a *Weltanschauung* or world-view, since this assumes a coherence and cohesiveness to a set of ideas. Thus, we might discuss the 'Romantic world-view' or the 'Elizabethan world-view', which is the philosophical and cultural underpinning of a particular group of people. Instead, an episteme consists of the sum total of the discursive structures which come about as a result of the interaction of the range of discourses circulating and authorised at that particular time. Thus, an episteme includes the range of methodologies which a culture draws on as self-evident in order to be able to think about certain subjects. Foucault shows that within certain periods there is a tendency to structure thinking about a subject in a particular way and to map out certain procedures and supports for thinking. So, for example, within the set of epistemes available within the Victorian era, scientific thought was characterised by a tendency to produce detailed tables, to label and systematise seemingly heterogeneous materials into very rigidly defined systems of classification. Consider this table from Brown's *The Races of Mankind* (1873–9).

Tschudi table of Peruvian Mongrelity illustrating the mongrel character of the Spanish American population of Peru:

Parents	Children
White father and negro mother	mulatto
White father and Indian mother	mestiza
Indian father and negro mother	chino
White father and mulatto mother	cuarteron
White father and mestiza mother	creole (pale brownish complexion)
White father and chino mother	chino–blanco
White father and cuarterona mother	quintero
White father and quintera mother	white
Negro father and Indian mother	zambo
Negro father and mulatto mother	zambo–negro
Negro father and mestiza mother	mulatto–oscura
Negro father and chino mother	zambo–chino

Negro father and zamba mother	zambo–negro
	(perfectly black)

. . .

and so on for thirty-two different 'crosses' of white, Indian and 'Negro'.

(cited in Young, 1995: 176)

For Victorians, this way of thinking about the world appeared the 'natural' way to describe racial difference, whereas when we look at these nineteenth-century classifications of racial distinctions they seem pathological in their excessive detail and scrupulous systematicity. We are alienated because here people are classified in the same way as dogs or horses might be classified, in terms of their breeding stock and the 'purity' of their lineage. As Young has shown, the same system of classification for hybridity in plants and cross-breeding in animals was transferred to the description of indigenous people (Young, 1995). But we are also distanced from this concern with charting in such meticulous detail the constituents of a field of knowledge, since this form of thinking has now been superseded by other ways of organising knowledge and information.[2] Within late twentieth-century Western thought, it is not assumed that you will grasp the essence of a subject, in this case, racial difference, merely by accumulating large amounts of data relating to the subject and organising this material into tabular form.

Foucault suggests that there are epistemic breaks, that is, at certain moments in a culture, there are discontinuous developments in discursive structures, so that for the Victorians the tabular representation of reality seemed entirely natural, whereas in the twentieth century this method of representation has begun to seem unusual. A further example that Foucault offers is of the significance given to events in relation to a divine order. Within Early Modern Europe, every event was interpreted according to a system of thought which linked the mundane world with the supernatural or religious order. Thus, what would now be classified as a natural phenomenon, such as a severe storm, would then be classified in terms of its significance in this wider symbolic system, perhaps as a portent or as a sign of divine displeasure. Events took their meaning from their place within this cosmological system, whereas in late twentieth-century Europe, no wider supernatural significance is attributed to storms. The constituents of this particular form of knowledge have changed; and whereas we would normally see this as due to the advance of scientific and secular thinking, Foucault proposes that our own systems of knowledge constituting current epistemes will appear equally as contrived and alien to future generations. It is easier to examine the epistemes that were current in past periods and past cultures precisely because the machinery of thinking within the contemporary culture is so naturalised.

This notion of the discontinuity of discourse enabled Foucault to counter the idea of the progress of cultures; rather than European history being seen as a progression from ignorance to greater truth, where previous stages along the road to the present could be viewed only in relation to the improved present, he suggested that in fact intellectual history should be seen as simply a series of lurches from one system of classification and representation to another. In this sense, Foucault differs in his thinking from both conservative and Marxist accounts of history; for central to both of these is the notion of improvement and progress: for conservatives greater scientific knowledge brings inevitable improvement to humankind; for Marxists, revolutionary change can only bring about improvement to the conditions of the working classes. This is perhaps where Foucault has most influenced postmodern thinking, for this Utopian notion of history is very much embedded in forms of thought. Indeed, when Catherine Belsey tried to explain her move away from a Marxist feminist position to what she called a materialist feminist position, she did so in Foucauldian terms: because of problems in mapping out the possible Utopias and clear goals which could be achieved by feminism, because of lack of consensus on what those might be, Belsey decided that the model of history – the grand narrative – which is an essential part of Marxist thought, would have to be discarded (Belsey, 1992). When she considered the advances which had been made within the past twenty years in relation to women's rights, she felt that it was necessary also to give some consideration to the areas in which women's rights had deteriorated. The model of a seamless progression of events towards an improved future disallows the consideration of such deterioration. A Foucauldian discontinuous model of history simply charts the shifts which take place within the machinery of thinking.

THE STATEMENT

Epistemes are constructed from sets of statements (énoncé) grouped into different discourses or discursive frameworks. Let us now consider what a statement is, as the primary building block of a discourse. Dreyfus and Rabinow state: 'The statement is neither an utterance nor a proposition, neither a psychological nor a logical entity, neither an event nor an ideal form' (Dreyfus and Rabinow, 1982: 45). A statement is not an utterance, in the sense that one sentence can actually function as several different statements, depending upon which discursive context it appears in. As Foucault puts it:

> At a certain scale of micro-history, one may consider that an affirmation like 'species evolve' forms the same statement in Darwin and in Simpson; at a finer level, and considering more limited fields of use ('neo-Darwinism' as opposed to the Darwinian system itself) we are presented with different statements. The constancy of the statement, the preservation of its identity through the unique events of the enunciations, its duplication through the identity of the forms is constituted by the functioning of the field of use in which it is placed.
>
> (Foucault, 1972: 104)

Dreyfus and Rabinow explain that several different utterances can, in fact, constitute one single statement, as when an airline steward makes the same announcement in several different languages. They go on to say: 'Maps can be statements, if they are representations of a geographical area, and even a picture of the layout of a typewriter keyboard can be a statement if it appears in a manual as a representation of the way the letters of a keyboard are standardly arranged' (Dreyfus and Rabinow, 1982: 45). Statements do seem to bear a striking similarity to the speech acts described by John Searle (1979) and John Austin (1962), although perhaps speech act theorists are more concerned with the force of an utterance, the way that an utterance is understood and acted on, than is Foucault.[3] Statements are for him those utterances which have some institutional force and which are thus validated by some form of authority – those utterances which for him would be classified as 'in the true': 'It is always possible one could speak the truth in a void; one would only be in the true, however, if one obeyed the rules of some discursive "police" which would have to be reactivated every time one spoke' (Foucault, 1972: 224). Those utterances and texts which make some form of truth-claim (and how many do not?) and which are ratified as knowledge can be classified as statements. In a sense, statements could be considered 'serious' speech acts (Dreyfus and Rabinow, 1982: 48). Foucault's archaeological analysis is concerned with the systems of support which govern the production and the ordering of these statements and, more importantly perhaps, the systems whereby other utterances are excluded from the position of being 'in the true' and therefore being classified as statements.

THE DISCOURSE/DISCOURSES

As I have tried to make clear in this chapter, there is an important distinction in Foucault's work to be made between discourse as a whole, which is the set of rules and procedures for the production of particular discourses, and those discourses or groups of statements themselves. A discourse is a set of sanctioned statements which have some institutionalised force, which means that they have a profound influence on the way that individuals act and think. What constitutes the boundaries of a discourse is very unclear. However, we can say that discourses are those groupings of statements which have similar force – that is, they are grouped together because of some institutional pressure, because of a similarity of provenance or context, or because they act in a similar way. Thus, for example, the discourse of middle-class femininity in the nineteenth century consisted of the set of heterogeneous statements (i.e., those utterances, texts, gestures, behaviour which were accepted as describing the essence of Victorian womanhood: humility, sympathy, selflessness) and which in fact constituted the parameters within which middle-class women could work out their own sense of identity. There were other discourses which challenged this knowledge (for example, the discourses of feminism), but this discourse of femininity was the type of knowledge that was sanctioned by many of the institutions within the Victorian era – the Church, the education system and so on – and which acted together to produce the boundaries of the possible forms of middle-class womanhood. It is this concern with the constituents of discourses which has received most critical attention and which perhaps has proved most useful to cultural and critical theorists, as I show in Chapters 4 and 5 on feminist theory and post-colonial theory. Foucault himself is less interested in statements in and of themselves than in the way they coalesce into discourses or discursive formations and take some of their force from such groupings.

THE ARCHIVE

Another discursive structure which Foucault isolated is the archive: Foucault describes the archive in the following terms: 'I mean the set of rules which at a given period and for a definite society defined: 1) the limits and forms of expressibility; 2) the limits of forms of conservation; 3) the limits and forms of memory; and 4) the limits and forms of reactivation' (Foucault, 1978: 14–15). In this sense, the notion of the archive can be seen to be working alongside the notion of the episteme, and can perhaps can be best apprehended through an analysis of Foucault's later work in his essay 'The order of discourse', which I discuss below. For the moment, an archive should be seen as the set of discursive mechanisms which limit what can be said, in what form and what is counted as worth knowing and remembering. It is this sense of limitation or exclusion which I would like to consider now in more detail, since it is crucial to the understanding of the constitution of discursive structures.

EXCLUSIONS WITHIN DISCOURSE

As well as attempting to define the way that discursive structures map out what we can say and what we can consider as legitimate knowledge, Foucault's article entitled 'The order of discourse' (1981) also discusses the difficulties of inserting oneself within a discourse, of starting to speak. 'The order of discourse' was originally given as an open lecture at the prestigious College de France where Foucault was obliged to give a once-yearly public lecture. Here Foucault was having to present an academic lecture which was also accessible to an audience containing a wide variety of people. He comments:

> I think a good many people have a similar desire to be freed
> from the obligation to begin, a similar desire to be on the other
> side of discourse from the outset, without having to consider

from the outside what might be strange, frightening, and perhaps maleficent about it. To this very common wish, the institution's reply is ironic, since it solemnises beginnings, surrounds them with a circle of attention and silence, and imposes ritualised forms on them, as if to make them more easily recognisable from a distance.

(Foucault, 1981: 51)

The beginning of a lecture in such a prestigious setting would generally be marked by introductions and by the recitation of the credentials of the speaker, giving that speaker credibility and the right to speak, the right to be considered worth listening to, the right to have all other voices silenced. But what Foucault is isolating here is that, even when the entry into discourse is ritualised in this way, it cannot quite overcome the way in which discourse evades these attempts to regulate it.

In 'The order of discourse' Foucault discusses the way that discourse is regulated by institutions in order to ward off some of its dangers. He describes the processes of exclusion which operate on discourse to limit what can be said and what can be counted as knowledge. The first of the procedures of exclusion he calls 'prohibition' or taboo: there are certain subjects which it is difficult to discuss within Western societies, such as death and sex. Within British culture many people have remarked that they have felt shunned and avoided by even their closest friends if their partner has died, because of the perceived difficulty of talking about death, and the lack of vocabulary in English to express one's feelings without sounding either hackneyed, insincere or overly formal. Within other cultures, and in the past in Britain, death was a subject which was discussed openly and which had a wide range of supports, i.e., material practices, rituals and artefacts which made it possible to talk about. In some cultures, such as Mexico, there is a proliferation of discourses around death. And indeed, within Victorian Britain there was an array of statements, artefacts and practices which would now be considered morbid or sentimental, but which allowed discussion of death and mourning.

Within Victorian Britain, it was very difficult to discuss sex openly and remain respectable, and sexual subjects were avoided at all costs within 'polite' society and mixed groups. Some of the societies which British subjects encountered within the colonial relationship had very different views on sexuality; for example, in India, as Macmillan notes:

> some temples had carvings which were obscene (or erotic, depending on your point of view). Memsahibs who went sightseeing were carefully steered away from them by their escorts; indeed a popular nineteenth century guidebook advised tipping local guides at a particularly notorious temple so that they would not call attention to shocking scenes.
>
> (Macmillan, 1988: 105)

There is nothing intrinsic to these subjects which makes them difficult to talk about, but for British culture, particularly within the Victorian period, it seemed self-evident that these were difficult topics. It is simply a discursive and institutional limitation which becomes habitual within particular cultures at certain periods. Once a subject is tabooed, that status begins to feel self-evident.

A second exclusion on what can be said centres around the discourse of those who are considered insane and therefore not rational. Foucault argues that in different historical periods, the speech of the mad person was considered either to be on the level of divine insight, or totally meaningless. In twentieth-century Britain the language of schizophrenics, for example, is not given credence, so that when seemingly 'mad' people speak, they are not heeded; if they make requests for particular types of treatment which are not sanctioned by those in authority they are generally ignored. It is assumed that the wishes and views of 'rational' people, such as doctors and social workers, carry more weight.

The third exclusion which maps out what can count as a statement and therefore part of a discursive framework is the division between knowledge which is perceived to be true and that which is considered to be false. Foucault charts the history of this division, stating that for Greeks in the sixth century, the content of a statement was no guarantee of its being true; rather, the circumstances under which it was said were of prime importance: 'a day came when the truth was displaced from the ritualised efficacious and just act of enunciation, towards the utterance itself, its meaning, its form, its object, its relation to its reference' (Foucault, 1981: 54). Foucault calls this transition a movement towards the 'will to truth', 'which imposed on the knowing subject, and in some sense prior to all experience, a certain position, a certain gaze and a certain function (to see rather than to read, to verify rather than to make commentaries on)' (Foucault, 1981: 55).

An illustration of this shift within Western cultures can be found in the work of Lennard Davis, who has shown that within the eighteenth century there was a transition from a certain laxity towards the division between fact and fiction, truth and falsehood, to an obsessive and legalistic compartmentalising of the division (Davis, 1983). With the beginning of the production of 'news', that is, texts which purported to be recent, accurate representations of noteworthy events rather than representations of events which had a moral, symbolic or wider religious significance, there began to be forged a division between truth and falsehood within the public domain which was supported and enacted through government intervention, through the introduction of libel laws and stamp duties on certain types of publications. This had a far-reaching effect on the production of texts in general, and it is at this time that the distinction between novels and 'factual' accounts begins to be made. Foucault demonstrates that this will to truth is supported by a range of institutions: educational establishments, publishing houses, legal institutions, libraries, and so on, to the point that it is almost impossible to question this obsession with the truth and the factual.[4] We assume that this is necessarily a distinction which must guide our thinking. Foucault shows the way that this led in literature within the nineteenth and early twentieth centuries to an obsession with *vraisemblance*, to demonstrating that what was written was a 'copy' of external reality. This concern to produce 'true' representations seems to many self-evident, and the search for 'truth' seems to some a possible goal for academic study. Whilst we often experience this will-to-truth as 'a richness, a fecundity, a gentle and insidiously universal force ... we are unaware of the ... prodigious machinery designed to exclude' (Foucault, 1981: 56). Exclusion is, in essence, paradoxically, one of the most important ways in which discourse is produced.

CIRCULATION OF DISCOURSES

In addition to these exclusionary procedures, Foucault remarks that the constitution of discourses also has internal mechanisms, which keep certain discourses in existence. The first of these circulatory mechanisms is commentary. Those discourses which are commented upon by others are the discourses which we consider to have validity and worth:

> we may suspect that there is in all societies, with great consistency, a kind of gradation among discourses: those which are said in the ordinary course of days and exchanges, and which vanish as soon as they have been pronounced; and those which give rise to a certain number of new speech acts which take them up, transform them or speak of them, in short, those discourses which, over and above their formulation, are said indefinitely, remain said, and are to be said again.
>
> (ibid.: 57)

The Bible (itself considered by some to be a set of commentaries) could be considered a text of this nature, upon which commentaries have been written and will continue to be written; in a sense, these commentaries keep the Bible in existence, ensure that it keeps in circulation as legitimate knowledge. Commentary attributes richness, density and permanence to the text at the very moment when it is creating those values by the act of commentary. But this is not an entirely selfless act:

> commentary's role . . . is to say at last what was silently articulated 'beyond' the text. By a paradox which it always displaces but which it never escapes, the commentary must say for the first time, what had, nonetheless, already been said, and must tirelessly repeat what had, however, never been said.
>
> (ibid.: 58)

This reminds one of the types of strategies adopted by more conventional literary critics when they attempted to articulate the true meaning of a literary text. New Critics, for example, felt that they had to produce a new, better, more comprehensive interpretation of the literary text, whilst arguing that this meaning was embedded in the text already, waiting to be discovered by a particularly skilled reader or critic. Within a Foucauldian view, this process of trying to 'discover' the 'real' meaning of the text is simply an illusory practice, which keeps texts in circulation.

This process whereby texts are kept in circulation by commentary on them is particularly important to consider within the sphere of literary criticism within universities and schools. Critical analysis by theorists is thus not a simple act of research but, as feminist theorists have shown, has an effect on which texts are considered worthy of publication and which ones are then maintained in print. All researchers within literary studies recognise that one accrues status to oneself by working on valued texts: that is, canonical primary texts and/or theoretically complex works. Because of this tendency to work on canonical texts, those texts which have been excluded from the canon tend not to be seen as worthy of analysis. Thus, feminist critics in the 1960s not only had difficulty accessing early texts by women, they also had difficulties in establishing the legitimacy of such study (Showalter, 1977). Non-canonical texts are often not in print and are therefore difficult for the student or researcher to access, and lecturers are loath to include them on reading lists. Thus, commentary serves not only to ensure that certain texts will always be in print, will always be taught in educational establishments and will always be worked upon by researchers, but it also makes it very difficult to institute the analysis of those texts about which little has been written.

A second internal regulator of discourse is the notion of the academic discipline: this is a larger-order discursive grouping which determines what can be said and regarded as factual or true within a given domain. Thus, each discipline will determine what methods, form of propositions and arguments, and domain of objects will be considered to be true. This set of structures allows for new propositions to be articulated, but only within certain discursive limits. Foucault would argue that the structures of disciplines exclude more propositions than they enable (as all who have attempted to carry out interdisciplinary work will have found). Even if your research work is factually accurate or insightful, if it does not accord with the form and content of particular disciplines it is likely to be disregarded, or to be regarded as non-academic or popular. Disciplines allow people to speak 'in the true', that is, within the realm of what is considered true within that discipline, but they also exclude from consideration other knowledges which might have been possible. For example, if an archaeologist writes an academic paper, because of disciplinary structures, their focus of study would necessarily be on human society and change; but archaeologists often unearth data which could more readily be considered to be the result of environmental change rather than of human acts. If an archaeologist encounters a site where there is evidence of soil erosion or fire damage, they are likely to interpret those traces as evidence of human activity: humans planted crops and caused the soil to erode; humans used fire to clear a site of trees. If a physical geographer encountered the same traces in a site, they would be more likely to see them as evidence of environmental activity: rivers eroded the soil; the site is subject to spontaneous fire damage. Thus, the discipline in this case determines how this data is classified. Disciplinary structures do not simply demarcate certain types of knowledge as belonging to particular domains, but also lead to the construction of distinct methodologies for analysis, and even within university campuses to buildings devoted to each discipline, so that philosophers, psychologists, linguists and semioticians who are all engaged in the study of the same object – language – do not in fact discuss their perspectives with each other.

Foucault focuses finally on the rarefaction of discourse as an internal discursive constraint. What he means by rarefaction is the surprising fact that although the utterances which could be produced by any one person are theoretically infinite, in fact, they are remarkably repetitive and remain within certain socially agreed-upon boundaries. In theory, any person could utter anything that they wanted to, but, firstly, people tend to remain, in the choice of their topics of conversation and in the words that they choose, fairly restricted by societal and personal norms, and secondly, people tend to be fairly restricted in terms of the construction of their own desires and needs. So what we find ourselves wanting to say falls within fairly predictable and restricted sets of parameters. An analogy might be with the fashion system: there are a limited number of garment styles, fabrics and colours available in the shops for us to buy. We structure our desires about the type of image of ourselves which we would like to project within the boundaries of what is available to us. Those choices we make about clothes nevertheless *feel* personal. Foucault would suggest that these limits are set up by discursive limits; we speak and act within the bounds of what discourses map out for us. We do not, for example, wear no trousers, unless wearing no trousers has been established as discursively acceptable and possible. An ideological analysis of the fashion industry would focus on the interests which are served by this limitation of the possibilities of expression, and Foucault is certainly clear that discursive limitations are those which are sanctioned by an institution of some kind. He is less concerned, however, with the interests which are served by these limitations than he is with the effects on expression that these limitations have.

Discourse is bounded about by rituals which limit the number of people who can utter certain types of utterance: for example, only a priest or registrar can legally marry a couple; only the monarch can open Parliament. If someone who is not sanctioned uttered the same words, the statement would not have an effect; thus, an actor who 'marries' someone on stage is not legally married to them. Foucault asks: 'What, after all, is an education system, other than a ritualization of speech, a qualification and fixing of the roles for speaking subjects, the constitution of a doctrinal group, however diffuse, a distribution and an appropriation of discourse with its powers and knowledges?' (Foucault, 1981: 64) Thus, rather than the education system being seen as an enlightening institution where free enquiry after the truth is encouraged, Foucault sees it rather as simply a form of regulation of discourse. There are strict speaking rights within educational institutions (for example, only the lecturer speaks within a lecture and all other speech is seen as aberrant unless sanctioned by the lecturer), and there are also strict rules about what can pass for knowledge (those attempts to express ideas which do not refer to past knowledge, and which are not expressed in the conventional format of the essay or the thesis, are generally stigmatised and are classified as failures).

Conversely, those forms of knowledge which accurately obey the rules of discourse will be ratified. An example of this is a recent spoof academic paper which created a scandal when it transpired, after it had been published, that the paper was in fact a hoax. The paper was entitled 'Transgressing the boundaries:

towards a transformative hermeneutics of quantum gravity' and was written by an American, the physicist Alan Sokal of New York University. It was submitted to the cultural studies journal *Social Text* as a spoof. Sokal wished to prove the vacuousness of cultural studies by publishing an article which was in essence meaningless, but which would gesture in the direction of citing the 'correct' theorists, and making the 'right' arguments to fit in with the current orthodoxy within cultural studies. It was accepted, since, as Peter Jones puts it, 'It spoke the lingo. That was all that counted. Evaluating the argument was of no interest' (Jones, 1996: 16). Whilst this is clearly an overstatement, the article was indeed accepted for publication because it obeyed the discursive rules prevalent in that discipline.

What makes Foucault's analysis of discourse in 'The order of discourse' so insightful is that he focuses on constraint – the way that we operate within discursive limits – rather than assuming that people are free to express whatever they wish. This focus on constraint may be seen as inherently negative, but when taken together with his later work in *The History of Sexuality*, mentioned in the previous chapter, this sense of constraint can be seen as productive as well as limiting. It is only through this process of constraint that knowledge can be produced.

Foucault's analysis of the author is also important in analysing the structures of discourse, since the author ceases to be the ratifier of the meaning of the text, but becomes a form of organisation for groups of texts. The author is no longer 'the speaking individual who pronounced or wrote a text, but . . . a principle of grouping of discourses, conceived as the unity and origin of their meaning' (Foucault, 1981: 58). Literary critics often use the notion of the author to impose a sense of order and a set of restricted concerns on a range of texts which in fact have little in common. Both Barthes and Foucault proposed the 'death' of the author, suggesting a shift away from a concern with the author herself, to a concern with: in Barthes' case, the role of the reader in the production of an interpretation of a text, and in Foucault's case, the function of the author in the process of making global statements about diverse texts (Foucault, 1980b; Barthes, 1986). Foucault examines the way that some discourses have authors whilst for others the concept of authorship is almost irrelevant; a legal document is not authored, since its authority springs from the institution, the government who sanctions it, rather than from the individual who wrote and edited it. An advertisement is not authored because it is seen as ephemeral and created by groups/teams of people rather than one single person. But literary texts are perhaps the texts which are most clearly categorised as authored texts, even though their creative ownership is problematic, since literary texts are formed more than any other texts in reaction to and within the constraints set up by other literary texts. Literary texts are, also, perhaps the most intertextual of all texts, referring to other texts in terms of literary allusion, and in terms of their formal structures (narrative voice, plot, character, and so on), and yet these are the texts where the creativity of a single author is held to be paramount. Nineteenth-century Romantic notions of the creative artist inform our sense of literary authorship. As Diane Macdonnell states: 'The concept of an "author" as a free creative source of the meaning of a book belongs to the legal and educational forms of the liberal humanist discourse that emerged in the late eighteenth and early nineteenth centuries; it is not a concept that exists within discourses that have developed recently' (Macdonnell, 1986: 3). Foucault questions the notion of creativity, arguing that it is rare for something original to be said, and even when a new idea is produced, it is produced within the constraints of what has previously been thought; furthermore, when a new idea is developed, Foucault questions the idea of ownership – there are so many other factors involved in the production of new ideas than the person themselves. Thus, a Foucauldian analysis would focus on the conditions of acceptance of new ideas and would perhaps attempt to analyse those ideas and inventions which were not sanctioned by a society and which were not classified by society as acceptable within its frames of reference.

An example of this would be the ideas of Francis Bacon, who noticed that the coasts of America and Eurasia seemed to fit into one another, and he assumed that at one time these two land masses had been joined together, thus prefiguring by four centuries the theory of plate tectonics. What Bacon lacked was a way of explaining the mechanism whereby such a movement might have taken place. His idea about the relation between the two coastlines was therefore disregarded; in scientific discourse it is not acceptable either to be so novel or to be right but for the wrong reasons.

Foucault is not arguing that there are no creative individuals. He is arguing instead that all individuals are potentially creative within the discursive constraints which enable ideas and texts to be produced. Most people have their creativity sapped at a very early age by society's pressures on them to conform through the education system. Perhaps he is questioning the simple assumption that the population is divided into a very tiny group of geniuses, such as Einstein, Shakespeare and da Vinci, and the rest of the population, who are not capable of creative thought (thought which challenges the parameters of the discursive constraints).

Rather than focusing on the author, Foucault focuses instead on the author-function, that principle of organisation which operates to group together disparate texts which often have very few common features. Thus, for example, Jane Austen's oeuvre is given a coherence and spoken of in terms of progression from the early novels to the later novels, and epithets such as 'immature' and 'mature' are used to describe this progress. In a similar fashion, Shakespeare's works are grouped together and discussed in terms of their common stylistic features, even though the authorship of some of the plays and poems is in doubt. This narrative of progress and the notion of an oeuvre is one which Foucault questions, since he asks whether this is in fact an order which we impose on the text given our knowledge of biographical information. In terms of literary texts, Foucault's critique of the author is insightful, since it enables us to move away from analysing texts in terms of the author's life, which for Foucault would be another and different set of texts.

All of these mechanisms for the structuring, constraining and circulation of information have a similar effect: they bring about the production of discourse, but only certain types of discourse. In a sense, they ensure that what can be said and what can be perceived to count as knowledge is very limited and occurs within certain very clearly delimited and recognised bounds. This ensures that the knowledge produced within a particular period has a certain homogeneity. That is not to suggest that all of the individuals existing within a certain era agree on a particular view of the world, but simply that all of the sanctioned utterances and texts are produced within similar discursive constraints.

CONCLUSIONS

What we can draw from this structuralist phase within both Barthes' and Foucault's work on discursive structures is the sense of discourse being composed of a set of unwritten regulations. The rules for the production of discourse do not seem necessarily to be composed by any one person, or group of people, and do not seem to be produced in the interests of any particular group, although they may in fact serve those interests. This arbitrariness of discursive structures is, for many, disconcerting; here we have the sense of our thoughts and utterances not simply springing from our own individual will/volition; instead we see that what we can express and what we think we might want to express is constrained by systems and rules which are in some senses beyond human control. These systems are ones which we are not necessarily aware of, and it is only through the type of archaeological work which Foucault and Barthes have initiated that we can begin to be aware of the frameworks within which discourse is produced and within which we construct our utterances and thoughts. Post-structuralist and postmodernist theory has largely undermined much of the theoretical underpinning of structuralism, questioning the existence of structures as a whole. However, this early work by Barthes and Foucault was fundamental in forcing us to consider the provenance of the very apparatus within which we think.

NOTES

1   I give a fuller definition of the statement later in this chapter.
2   Norman Fairclough's work on change in discursive structures is interesting in this respect, since he gives detailed accounts of small-scale change to current epistemes (Fairclough, 1992b).
3   Foucault is not concerned with this pragmatic understanding of individual utterances; far more than Austin or Searle, it is not individual utterances which are his focus of attention, but the rules which govern the production of utterances in general, and the limits of what can be expressed (see Searle, 1979).
4   Even the coining of the term 'factional' masks our sense of unease in the twentieth century with texts which do not fit easily into one category or another.

4

FEMINIST THEORY AND DISCOURSE THEORY

The next two chapters will explore two areas of research where theorists have tried to modify Foucault's work on discourse: in both of these areas (in this chapter, feminist theory, and in the next chapter, colonial and post-colonial discourse theory) theorists have tried to make the concept of discourse work to serve political ends, and thus they have had to strive to make some of the political potential of the theorising of discourse more overt than Foucault did.

Feminist theory has drawn heavily on Foucault's discourse theory work. Recently, there have been a number of feminist theoretical works which have explored the use of the term discourse for feminist ends (for example Diamond and Quinby, 1988; Smith, 1990; Mills, 1991; Sawicki, 1991; McNay, 1992). Without becoming overly embroiled in feminist theoretical debates about the uses to which Foucault's work can be put, this chapter aims to examine the uses which feminist theory has made of the term discourse, transforming it from its original Foucauldian usage.

This chapter discusses the ways in which discourse as a term can be put to use in analysis and focuses on a number of short texts to demonstrate the potential of discourse theory for feminist analysis.

It might seem paradoxical to use Foucault's work within feminist theory, since, as Meaghan Morris has shown, Foucault's work is not easily translatable into feminist concerns; his work on sexuality only touches marginally on the question of female hysteria, and he is certainly not a theorist who addresses gender issues as they relate to women (Morris, 1979). In addition, because of the perceived difficulty of formulating a clear political agenda within Foucault's view of discourse, it may also seem paradoxical that his work has been so widely used in feminist theory. However, discourse theory has been particularly productive because of its concern with theorising power.

Feminist theorists are generally concerned to analyse power relations and the way that women as individuals and as members of groups negotiate relations of power. Recent feminist work has moved away from viewing women as simply an oppressed group, as victims of male domination, and has tried to formulate ways of analysing power as it manifests itself and as it is resisted in the relations of everyday life. As I showed in Chapter 2 on discourse and ideology, the way that discourse is conceptualised allows for this sense of the complexity of power relations. Foucault's analysis of power has been very influential with feminist theorists, since it seems to be possible to develop a model of power relations which is fairly complex and which can deal with other variables such as race and class without having to prioritise one of them over the others. Whereas hard-line Marxist theorists would still consider class to be the most important factor in the oppression of certain groups, and would consider gender simply as a form of secondary exploitation, a Foucauldian analysis would see class concerns integrated with concerns about gender (Cliff, 1984). People are not oppressed because of their class separately from their oppression because of race or gender, although one of those factors might feel dominant at any particular moment. In her discussion of the impossibility of separating gender, race and class when describing relations of power under imperialism, Anne McClintock puts it in the following way:

> imperialism cannot be understood without a theory of gender power. Gender power was not the superficial patina of empire, an ephemeral gloss over the more decisive mechanisms of class and race. Rather, gender dynamics were, from the outset, fundamental to the securing and maintenance of the imperial enterprise.

> (McClintock, 1995: 6–7)

Thus, gender is always already formed through the vectors of race and class.

Feminists have, since the 1960s, insisted on the fact that the 'personal is political'. This slogan is still in current usage for a number of reasons: firstly, mainstream political activity has not until recently seemed to concern itself with matters which it considers belong to the private sphere, i.e., childcare provision, domestic labour, sexual abuse, domestic violence and issues of reproductive rights. Furthermore, many feminists have come to view mainstream political activity (i.e., voting, lobbying, party politics, petitions, and so on) as ineffective in changing the really pressing problems in our lives. Finally, the phrase 'the personal is political' has resonance precisely because those problems which many women once considered to be their fault, e.g. conflicts around the allocation of responsibility over childcare and house-work, have come to be seen, in fact, as problems which are structural and therefore political, rather than simply individual matters to be negotiated with partners. This concern with redefining the scope of the political is one which Foucault has been drawn to. He states:

> To say that 'everything is political' is to recognise the omni-
> presence of relations of force and their immanence to a
> political field; but it is to set oneself the barely sketched task
> of unravelling this indefinite tangled skein.
>
> (Foucault, 1979b: 72)

Thus, Foucault's revising of the model of power relations is very useful for feminist theorists trying to reinscribe the 'political' into the private sphere and attempting to map out possible strategies for bringing about change within an increasingly complex system of power.

I would like to focus on certain concepts which feminist theorists have drawn from Foucault's work, and which have significantly modified our notion of what discourse is. The types of discourse which Foucault isolated and which have been used for feminist ends, which I will discuss here, are the confessional and the discourse of femininity. I then go on to consider women's access to discourse, and conflicts between discursive structures.

CONFESSIONAL DISCOURSE

The confessional is one of the types of discourse which Foucault has discussed in relation to disciplinary society which has been important for feminist theorists. In *Discipline and Punish* (1979a) he examines the changes which have taken place in the way that punishment for violations of the law is administered, from the medieval period until the present day. Within the medieval period, in order to encourage citizens to obey the law and to maintain the *status quo*, punishment was meted out to individuals publicly as a warning to others of the results of social deviance. Punishment was thus physically displayed upon the tortured, mutilated body of the 'criminal', on the bodies hanging from gibbets, the heads staked on city walls, and in the processes of hanging, drawing and quarter-ing. In present-day Western cultures, this type of punishment is no longer sanctioned; instead, moves are made to reform those who are categorised as criminals, and force them to internalise a disciplinary regime which will regulate their future behaviour.[1] Foucault argues that it is not only those who are judged to be criminals who are subdued by these disciplinary structures, but also the population as a whole. The regulatory regimes devised in prisons have been extended to other spheres such as the school, the church and the home, so that discipline is internalised by individuals and begins to be seen as self-discipline. One of the practices by which subjects are disciplined is the confessional.

The confessional is perhaps the discourse which displays the operation of power most clearly. Foucault describes the confessional in the following terms:

> The Christian West invented this astonishing constraint, which it imposed on everyone, to say everything in order to efface every-thing, to formulate even the least faults in an uninterrupted, desperate, exhaustive murmuring, from which nothing must escape.

> (Foucault, 1979c: 84)

This notion of confession has proved useful for feminist theorists who have analysed conduct literature and women's religious writings, and the relation between confessing and submitting to a relation of power. For Foucault, those who confessed and displayed themselves as compliant subjects, in the process constructed themselves as those compliant subjects. For example, psychoanalytic therapy would, for Foucault, seem to be the epitome of confessional discipline, whereby the subject internalised the problem as her own in the process of telling the therapist about her difficulties. The subject is turned into a 'case' in the process of inserting herself into the psychoanalytic confessional discourse. Feminist theorists have noted for some years that women tend to be categorised as mentally ill and to suffer from depression in far greater numbers than men; women are also more likely to be admitted to mental institutions than men for similar problems (Showalter, 1987). The confessional, where women talk about their difficulties, may be used as a way of dealing with these problems in ways which are not in the woman's interest. It may also be that these problems are not in fact difficulties which the woman alone faces, but may be due to the unreal demands which society places on women as a whole. Societal demands for certain types of body shape and certain types of compliant behaviour from women may result in behaviour such as anorexia, bulimia, depression and outbursts of anger, all of which may be classified by a therapist as aberrant.

But for some feminist theorists, the process of producing compliant subjects is not so simple. Even in the process of producing oneself as someone who has emotional difficulties, there can be possible sites of resistance produced at the same time; instead of seeing the difficulties as being one's own responsibility or fault, in the process of therapy one can begin to trace ways in which personal difficulties can be caused by larger societal forces and other individuals and social groups. Dorothy Smith, a feminist discourse theorist and sociologist, in her essay 'K is mentally ill', has located this construction of someone as mentally ill as a process which is determined by assessments of behaviour judged against discursive norms (Smith, 1990: 12–51). Precisely because it is a discursive procedure, it is open to revision and rewriting. Like all texts, the interpretation depends on the context within which the confession takes place. When therapy is undertaken within a general institutional setting, it may be the case that a woman may be constructed as mentally unstable and blame may be attributed to her for her emotional difficulties. However, within the context of feminist therapy, other interpretations may be placed on the material. Many feminists have seen the process of 'confessing', and thus locating oneself within a larger interest group or political group (such as feminists, or working-class women or lesbian women), as one whereby a certain amount of resistance to oppression may be generated. The 'consciousness-raising' groups of the 1960s and 1970s were very much about changing the context within which women 'confessed' to difficulties adjusting to societal demands. Telling others everything about your life was seen as a way of reframing that narrative so that different causes and different trajectories could be formulated. Thus, whilst feminist theorists see the confessional as potentially an oppressive form of inter-action, for example, where women are classified as mentally ill by male psychotherapists, there is a sense in which confession within particular politicised contexts may be empowering, setting stories of 'failure' and 'self-blame' into contexts where those same 'failings' can be seen to be structural problems with Western culture's demands on women (Baker-Miller, 1978; Eichenbaum and Orbach, 1982; Wilkinson, 1986).

To see the way in which feminist discourse theory has modified Foucault's theorising of the workings of the confessional, let us consider this extract from the diary of a seventeenth-century woman, Alice Thornton who writes after the death of her newly born son:

> 1658: The weakness of my body continued so great and long after my hard childbirth of my son that it brought me almost into a consumption, not expecting for many days together that I should at all recover. And when it was done, I was lame almost a quarter of a year of my left knee, that I got in my labour. But it was nothing to that which I have deserved from the hand of God if he, in much mercy, had not spared my life. The Lord make me truly remember his goodness and that I may never forget this above all, his mighty and stretched-out hand of deliverances to me, his poor creature, that I may extol and praise the Lord with all my soul and never let go my hope from the God of my salvation, but live the remainder of the life he gives me to his honour and glory.
>
> (Thornton cited in Graham *et al.*, 1989: 154)

In a classic Foucauldian analysis, this would be classified as a confessional, displaying and constructing a compliant subject who accepts all difficulties as a sign of the need for greater subjection to the power of God. The reports which she gives of her illness and suffering are only the vehicles for the display of her own worthlessness in relation to this greater power, who is shown to be supremely merciful, even when he appears to be most cruel. However, in a feminist discourse theory analysis, there is a sense in which this display is seen to be precarious. We can see that, in producing accounts of this kind, the writer constructs herself as a devout subject, i.e., as a conforming member of a religious group, and this is already a position of some strength within the society she lived where only 'good' (i.e., obedient and devout) female subjects were revered.[2] However, at the same time, we can also see that the amount of work which is required to turn this into an account of God's grace is substantial; Alice Thornton's account as a whole details at some length the mishaps which befell her: the deaths in the family, the loss of her child, her illness. These events could be viewed as signs of God's displeasure with her for sin, for example. She gains a certain amount of personal power within discourse through being able to force these problems to become, despite everything, signs of God's goodness and mercy rather than his malevolence. The very fact of a woman 'speaking out', albeit within the seemingly private sphere of the diary, is in itself, given the constraints of the seventeenth century, highly subversive. Thus, rather than being a position simply of the display of compliance, there are possibilities within the discourse of the confessional to accrue power to oneself. Through the act of writing a confessional, it is possible to bring oneself and one's actions into alignment with God and hence a position of strength. These autobiographical writings align the subject with the power of God, through displaying herself as the object of God's mercy. Furthermore, diaries within the seventeenth century were often written not simply to display oneself as a 'good' subject but to try to set the record straight, to tell the truth. Whilst that notion of the truth is problematic in Foucauldian terms, as we saw when examining the relation of truth and knowledge in Chapters 1 and 3, it is possible for women to write in seemingly compliant ways yet still be making powerful strategic interventions in their own self-presentations and in their interactions with others in the world.

Dorothy Smith's (1990) work has made a significant contribution to current theorising of discourse, since she sees discourse less as something to which one is subjected than as a vehicle which is used by subjects to work out interpersonal relationships, complying with certain elements and actively opposing others. As I showed in Chapter 3, whilst, for many feminists, the very anonymity of discursive structures is a theoretical problem, since it does not allow you to track down the cause of an action or event easily, there is a sense in which it is still possible to locate individual agency without submitting either to extreme interpretations of Foucault's views of discourse as disembodied or to naive formulations of individualism. For, as Smith insists, texts are not somehow divorced from social contexts and individual participants simply because we analyse them in terms of their discursive structures. It is worth considering a fairly lengthy quotation from Smith to explore further this sense of the social embeddedness of discourse:

> The notion of discourse displaces the analysis from the text as originating in writer or thinker, to the discourse itself as an ongoing intertextual process. In the context of Foucault's archaeology, the concept of discourse has some of the same force as structuralism in displacing the subject or reducing her to a mere bearer of systemic processes external to her. Analysis of the extended social relations of complex social processes requires that our concepts embrace properties and processes which cannot be attributed to or reduced to individual 'utterances' or 'speech acts'. Ongoing organisation and relations co-ordinating multiple sites are produced by actual individuals, but the forms of organisation are not intended or fully regulated by a set or sub-set of those individuals. Members of discourse

orient to the order of the discourse in talk, writing, creating images whether in texts or on their bodies, producing and determined by the ongoing order which is their concerted accomplishment and arises in the concerting.

(ibid.: 161–162)

In this treatment of discourse, Smith wants to achieve a more socially context-bound view of discourse, which is attentive to what individual subjects do within and through discursive structures, rather than assuming that discourses force us to behave in certain ways.

DISCOURSES OF FEMININITY AND HETEROSEXUALITY

I would like here to consider the way that discourse theory has proved useful to feminist theorists attempting to describe the structures of femininity and heterosexuality. If we consider Dorothy Smith's work on femininity as discourse, where women actively work out their subject positions and roles in the process of negotiating discursive constraints, we can see how drawing on the notion of discourse is a significant improvement from earlier feminist theorising, which saw femininity simply as an imposed ideological category and which thus tended to cast women as passive victims of oppression (see Mills, 1992b for a more detailed discussion of the differences between these two views of femininity).

Let us first consider the early feminist work in order to examine more adequately the advantages of discourse theory. Those feminists who see femininity as an ideology to which women are subjected tend to consider femininity as homogeneous, as affecting all women in the same way; ideology as a structure does not allow for relatively different effects to be experienced by different groups of women, and it does not allow that there might be different ideological structures for different classes or sexual orientations. Thus, a heterosexual female who considers herself feminine might engage in different behaviours from a lesbian who considers herself feminine. There might also be different outcomes and interpretations of these feminine behaviours: if a 'femme' lesbian dressed in soft feminine clothes, she might be considered a 'lipstick' lesbian, parodying heterosexual femininity, whereas a straight female might be interpreted as displaying submissiveness to males. It is also not clear within this ideological theorising why women should accept these structures of femininity, which are portrayed as limiting them, since, within this type of theorising, it is clearly not in their interests to do so.[3] Furthermore, this model of femininity gives no sense of how, if femininity is such a negative characteristic, it can be resisted, rather than simply rejected wholesale. The notion of femininity as a social construct is so rigid that it does not allow for the possibility of change and instead portrays women as passive recipients. It is assumed in this type of theorising that 'stereotypes of femininity . . . are constructs created by men' (Palmer, 1989: 33). However, in some sense, women as well as men are actively engaged in maintaining these discourses in place as well as trying to dismantle elements of them and replacing them with other more productive elements. Finally, femininity is handled in ideological analyses as only having one clear meaning; that is, a woman acting in a feminine way can only be interpreted as displaying weakness or deference.[4] Thus, theorists who have attempted to counter some of these negative views of femininity have only managed to do so by revaluing feminine characteristics; for example, Jean Baker-Miller argues that we should see the traits which constitute femininity (intuition, vulnerability, emotionalness) as a way forward for the construction of a better, more humane society (Baker-Miller, 1978). However, there is a sense in which the constituents of femininity are not so clearly coded in terms of their meaning as has been assumed.

Dorothy Smith (1990) has used the notion of a discourse of femininity in order to move away from this view of social constructs being imposed on passive female subjects. She stresses the fact that discourse structures are discontinuous; that is, they change over time because of women's resistance to them and because of changes in social structures. Also, since discourse is something that you *do* (rather than something to which you are subjected), engaging with discourses of femininity constitutes an interactional relation of power rather than an imposition of power. Femininity does not have a single meaning, but depends on a wide range of contextual features, such as perceived power relations, for its interpretation and effect. As Biddy Martin puts it: 'power . . . is the relation between pleasures, knowledge and power as they are produced and disciplined' (cited in Diamond and Quinby, 1988: 6). Discourse theory sees power as enacted within relationships and thus as something which can be contested at every moment and in every interaction. Smith explains:

> To explore femininity as discourse means a shift away from viewing it as a normative order, reproduced through socialisation, to which women are somehow subordinated. Rather femininity is addressed as a complex of actual relations vested in texts.
>
> (Smith, 1990: 163)

This textual/discursive nature of femininity makes it open to acts of reinterpretation and re-scripting.

Perhaps what makes this view of femininity as discourse so persuasive is that rather than seeing, for example, conduct books and advice manuals for women as being straightforward indicators or signs of the degree of women's oppression, instead, they can be seen as merely an indication of the scale of the problem posed by women and their resistance to being counselled in this way. The fact, for example, that there were a great number of conduct books written in the nineteenth century assures us that there was a fundamental and pressing problem with women's behaviour which these texts were attempting to overcome. It is clear that women were *not* the compliant subjects these books tried to produce. For example, if we consider the following passage from Thomas Broadhurst's *Advice to Young Ladies on the Improvement of the Mind and Conduct of Life* (1810), it becomes clear that the text displays the problems just as prominently as the supposed solution:

> She who is faithfully employed in discharging the various duties of a wife and daughter, a mother and a friend, is far more usefully occupied than one who, to the culpable neglect of the most important obligations, is daily absorbed by philosophic and literary speculations, or soaring aloft amidst the enchanted regions of fiction and romance.
>
> (cited in Armstrong and Tennenhouse, 1987: 106)

This advice may simply be seen as an instruction to young girls to be dutiful wives and mothers, but in the very act of encouraging certain types of behaviour the writer includes mention of the types of behaviour which he is trying to discourage. However, even he is unable to make them sound wholly unattractive. This passage is clearly an indication of the fact that literature and learning in general exerted a strong attraction for young women at this time, perhaps to the detriment of their performing their conventional duties as wives and mothers. Kate Flint echoes this view in her work on nineteenth-century women as readers, where reading itself is seen to be a sinful, dangerous activity with the power to corrupt and harm women. For example E. J. Tilt states in *On the Preservation of Health of Women at the Critical Periods of Life* (1851) that:

> Novels and romances, speaking generally, should be spurned, as capable of calling forth emotions of the same morbid description which, when habitually indulged in, exert a disastrous influence on the nervous system, sufficient to explain that frequency of hysteria and nervous diseases which we find among the highest classes.
>
> (cited in Flint, 1993: 58)

It is clear that reading is characterised as particularly dangerous to women because of the disruptions which were necessarily entailed when women became active, thinking subjects and agents who could choose whether or not to be wives and mothers. This development of the New Woman was one which was hedged about by a plethora of advice manuals signalling the perceived dangers to women's mental and physical health.

The discourses which circulated within the nineteenth century around the question of women and reading are simply evidence of the great difficulty which women found in inhabiting the discursive structures laid out for them which stressed their duties and obligations as wives and mothers and did not hold out space for them to negotiate their own pleasures. It is only these admonitory discourses which remind us of the fact that these discourses of advice were not successful (Flint, 1993). Rather than seeing the proliferation of advice manuals on women's conduct as evidence of women's oppression, we can see them, amongst other things, as indicators of women's resistance to those discourses. As I showed in Chapter 3, Foucault examined the discourses on masturbation amongst children in the nineteenth century and he found that rather than these advice manuals simply giving advice to parents as to how to prevent their children from masturbating, we can see them as perhaps structuring and in some cases initiating sexual behaviour amongst children. A similar problem is encountered in drugs education, where at the same time as warning adolescents about the dangers of drug usage, any drugs education campaign is also drawing the attention of those same individuals to the potential illicit pleasures of drugs. By portraying drug use as dangerous risk-taking behaviour, drugs education runs the risk of emphasising the aspect of drug use which appeals to adolescents intent on rebelling against the *status quo*. Many of the black-and-white, documentary-style posters produced by drugs education bodies to warn adolescents that they could die if they engage in drug taking are used by young people to reaffirm their sense of identity as drug users. Thus, whilst drug-awareness campaigns intend to prevent drug use, they often serve to create certain types of counter-cultural images of drug users. Therefore, discourses should not be interpreted at face value; individuals actively engage with discourses in order to forge particular positions of identity for themselves.

For Dorothy Smith, Western society is largely structured by the texts of social actions from which we learn a given set of terms and actions: 'learning how to "mean" with words correctly in [a] setting is learning how it is socially organised' (Smith, 1990: 166). She goes on to comment:

> Rather than an image of superstructure balanced over the layers of relations of production rather like the frosting on a cake, the concept of a discourse of femininity . . . envisages a web or cats-cradle of texts, stringing together and co-ordinating the multiple local and particular sites of the everyday/ everynight worlds of women and men with the market processes of the fashion, cosmetic, garment and publishing industries.
>
> (ibid.: 167)

In this sense, discourse is not an abstract set of textual practices but the grounds on which social relations are organised. Smith describes the way that discourse is the means through which social relations between individuals are negotiated. Where femininity as a discourse becomes most crucial is where it forms the focus of group activity by individuals – where women are not portrayed as simple dupes of an ideology, but rather as actively constructing positions for themselves, using discursive constructs:

> When the codes and images are viewed as women use, play with, break with and oppose them, the discourse of femininity appears not as a managed construct of the fashion industry manipulating people as puppets, but as an ongoing, unfolding,

historically evolving, social organisation in which women and sometimes men are actively at work.

(ibid.: 204)

In this way, women who seem to be displaying their femininity can be viewed as agents rather than simply as the passive victims of oppressive ideologies.

Femininity is thus a special form of textually mediated relation, that is, where texts mediate or are the focus or instigator of activities, for example, in conduct books or advice columns where the reader examines herself from the standpoint of a text. Problem pages in women's magazines are displays of women finding it difficult to negotiate discourses; these pages of problems offer solutions, but they are also important in the sense of their foregrounding the difficulty women often have inserting themselves 'correctly' within the perceived norms of feminine behaviour (Mills, 1995b). They negotiate relations also between women as individual subjects, since they help to establish positions for individual women within the reading community of the particular women's magazine.

For Smith, a woman partakes in the discourses of femininity by wearing feminine, soft clothes; 'she presents herself as text to be read using doctrines of femininity as interpretative schemata. They are read back into her as the underlying pattern to the "documents" of femininity she exhibits' (Smith, 1990: l77). However, even this analysis needs some modification, since this representation of femininity is primarily a heterosexual one. It assumes that the signals which the documents/clothes produce are understandable to all the decoders of the message. If we set this message outside of the discourse of heterosexual femininity, different messages are possible. Consider the 'lipstick lesbian' who dresses in a parodic feminine way in order to present herself as a certain type of sexual agent but also to destabilise heterosexual norms. In an article on gay and lesbian space, David Bell, John Binnie, Julia Cream and Gill Valentine state that:

> The excessive performance of masculinity and femininity within homosexual frames exposes not only the fabricated nature of heterosexuality but also its claims to authenticity. The 'macho' man and the 'femme' woman are not tautologies, but work to disrupt conventional assumptions surrounding the straight mapping of man/masculine and woman/feminine within heterosexual and homosexual constructs.
>
> (Bell *et al.*, 1994: 33)

They go on to suggest that 'lipstick style thus has the potential to make heterosexual women question how their own appearance is read, [and] to challenge how they see other women' (ibid.: 42). Thus, a feminine appearance cannot be interpreted simply as having one single meaning; femininity may have a number of different effects and functions, dependent on context.

A further advantage that feminist theorists have found in discourse theory has been in relation to the theorising of causality. In some senses, ideological criticism has had to posit an agency, the State, or larger structural institutions whose interests ideological practices served. Within this type of theorising, patriarchy – a rather amorphous, agentless term – was used to describe the type of society within which women are oppressed in the interests of men (see Walby, 1990 for a fuller discussion of theorising patriarchy). Discourse theorists find it more difficult to describe patriarchy; that is not to say that they do not believe in a system of discrimination which often works in the interests of males at the expense of females, but they do not consider that systems of discrimination work so smoothly. Discourse theorists do not deny the importance of institutional power (the power of the State, the judiciary, the police, and so on), since it is clear that roles are carved out for individuals by these institutions; but perhaps they are more concerned with mapping out the multiple sites where power is enacted and negotiated. Within discourse theory, it is possible to see that the practices which oppress women are not uniform, since women are not a homogeneous group; some women negotiate for themselves positions of institutionalised power and others accrue power to themselves by negotiating with the seemingly powerless positions which they have been allotted. There are a wide range of discursive and institutional structures which oppress women and which women in turn are either compliant with or resistant to. Thus, feminist analysis focuses on *discourses* rather than a single discourse as the cause or one of the determining factors in women's subjection. And these discourses, as I mentioned earlier, will be in conflict with other discourses, which will force them to change in structure and content and which will make available to women and to men spaces wherein they can resist and construct their own sense of self.

In attempting to theorise femininity, Sandra Bartky (1989) has addressed the question of the 'origins' of women's oppression and patriarchal power. She has used discourse theory to analyse anorexia, which she sees as simply the logical conclusion of the discursive structures of femininity. She sees anorexia as a discursive pressure on the female body. She describes the way that the female body is described in current magazines and advertisements as a disciplinary practice, in that the female body is subject to the need for control and work: 'the ideal body of femininity – and hence the feminine body subject – is constructed; in doing this they produce a "practised and subjected" body, that is, a body on which an inferior status has been inscribed' (Bartky, 1988: 71). Anorexia here is not viewed as an illness or as a mental aberration but rather as a series of disciplinary practices: 'The technologies of femininity are taken up and practised by women against a background of a pervasive sense of bodily deficiency; this accounts for what is often their compulsive or even ritualistic character' (ibid.: 71). What she wants to know is 'if what we have described is a genuine discipline – a system of micro-power that is essentially non-egalitarian and asymmetrical – who then are the disciplinarians? Who is the top sergeant in the disciplinary regime of femininity?' (ibid.: 76). She examines the possible options – the family, the law, the police, the media – and suggests that none of them wields 'the kind of authority that is typically invested in those who manage more straightforward disciplinary institutions. The disciplinary power that inscribes femininity in the female body is everywhere and it is nowhere; the disciplinarian is everyone and yet no one in particular' (ibid.: 76). Thus, whilst Foucault in his work on discipline and the body tends to locate the imposition of discipline within specific institutions – the school, the factory, the prison – Bartky is more concerned with the way that discursive structures are 'unbound', that is, not limited to institutional sources and sites. This has certain key effects for feminist theorising of patriarchy and for the formulation of patterns of resistance: 'The absence of a formal institutional structure and of authorities invested with the power to carry out institutional directives creates the impression that the production of femininity is either entirely voluntary or natural' (ibid.: 75). However, feminist analysis can locate the discursive work necessary for the production of femininity as 'natural' and can thus defamiliarise this discursive structure.

Bartky considers some of the sanctions which operate against women who refuse femininity or who cannot conform to the body type and disciplinary regime of femininity. She quotes several women whom she interviewed in the course of her work on anorexia:

> I felt so clumsy and huge. I would knock over furniture, bump into things, tip over chairs, not fit into VWs, especially when people were trying to crowd into the back seat. I felt I was taking up the whole room . . . I felt disgusting and like a slob. In the summer I felt hot and sweaty and I knew that people saw my sweat as evidence that I was too fat.

> I feel so terrible about the way I look that I cut off connection with my body. I operate from the neck up. I do not look in

mirrors. I do not want to spend time buying clothes. I do not want to spend time with make-up because it's painful for me to look at myself.

(cited in ibid.: 76–77)

What Bartky is trying to discover is, given the problems with this type of disciplinary structure, why it is that all women are not feminists. Thus, she is trying to discover the parameters of patriarchy, if she can still hold to such a unified concept, and the possibilities of resistance.

Christine White and I have shown in an article on discursive constraints and the construction of desire (Mills and White, forthcoming) that the categories and narratives which discourse constructs for subjects are not simply imposed, but are subject to negotiation by those subjects. It is the process of engaging with discursive structures that constitutes us as particular types of individuals or subject positions. Heterosexuality is a set of discursive constructs with which subjects interact, refusing certain elements and accepting others. Subjects always feel discomfort in their negotiations with these constructs and may interpret such discomfort as a sign of their own inadequacy or as the oppressiveness of society's views of women. Feminist heterosexuals may feel that they are critical of institutional heterosexuality which accords privilege to heterosexuals (such as pension rights, immigration rights), whilst denying those rights to those who are not heterosexual. They may also find that they need to resist assumptions made about heterosexuals by society as a whole; for example, that the female in a couple will be responsible for the housework and childcare, will earn less, will be less confident, will support her husband/partner, will follow him in his change of workplace, and so on. They may also have to counter certain assumptions made by lesbians about their relationships; for example, that heterosexual relationships are necessarily based on oppression. But they may also find that there are certain elements within the way that they negotiate the structures of heterosexual desire that are pleasurable. Thus, individual subjects should not be seen simply to adopt roles which are mapped out for them by discourses; rather, they experience discomfort with certain elements implicit in discourses, they find pleasure in some elements, they are openly critical about others. Individual subjects are constantly weighing up their own perception of their own position in relation to these discursive norms against what they assume other individuals or groups perceive their position to be. In this way, the process of finding a position for oneself within discourse is never fully achieved, but is rather one of constantly evaluating and considering one's position and, inevitably, constantly shifting one's perception of one's position and the wider discourse as a whole.

ACCESS TO DISCOURSE

Feminist theory is intensely involved in questions over access to discourse, since it is clear that women frequently do not have the same access as men to speaking rights, as has been amply documented by various studies (see Coates and Cameron, 1989; Tannen, 1990). A simple example of this is the way that women generally do not speak at weddings; it is very difficult for women to insert themselves as speaking subjects in such an environment when most of the formal speaking roles are designated as male (men give the speeches at the reception; men generally 'give the bride away'; men toast the bridesmaid and the bride; men read the telegrams, and so on) (Cameron, 1990). There are institutionalised constraints here which serve to silence women in terms of public speaking. This is not to suggest that women are simply incompetent speakers, but that discursive structures are sites where power struggles are played out. For example, it has often been noted that in mixed-sex conversations which take place in the public sphere, certain discursive rules prevail and they are generally those which are more in line with masculinist competitive norms of speech. So, in a board meeting or committee meeting, within this style of speech, each speaker tries to grab a turn at talk and tries to locate themselves within a hierarchy – this hierarchy is fixed on the basis of perceived power positions within the group (who earns the most, who has the best job, who is employed, but also who is most able to compete verbally and display verbal dexterity and wit). More co-operative speech norms, such as those which are principally engaged with in all-female friendship groups, are often not perceived by mixed groups of speakers as having value (Coates, 1989, 1995). Within co-operative speech styles, participants consider the ongoing flow of the talk to be more important than their own particular contribution to that talk; they may give up their own contribution in order to elicit a contribution from another member of the group who does not seem to be participating. Whilst feminist theorists such as Dale Spender (1980) have suggested that this disparity between the speech styles and the devaluing of women's speech patterns is due to a male conspiracy against women, this view of women's speech is currently being revised (Coates and Cameron, 1989; Mills, 1995b).

Discursive rules are always under constant negotiation and renegotiation. For example, in university seminar groups it is sometimes the case, in academic subjects where there are more males than females, that male students will tend to dominate, will speak more and will interrupt more frequently, whereas female students may not intervene so forcefully. In other academic subjects, where female students are in the majority, such as English literature or cultural studies, it is clear that the norms of discourse are being revised. In seminar groups where all of the students have the same access to knowledge about a subject, and where it is considered appropriate for women or men to know about that subject, women and men will tend to intervene in roughly similar ways. Much work on how people speak helps us to realise how closely tied in with notions of power is the issue of who speaks. If you alter one of the variables in the nexus of power relations, you will change the type and form of the speech which is produced. This revised view of power has helped feminist theorists to unravel the complexities of the power relations between men and women, and particularly helps us to understand differential access to discourse. But seeing co-operative and competitive talk as discourses which are differently valued enables us to reconsider the ways in which women's and men's speech are produced as different from one another. Thus, rather than assuming that men operate within one set of speech norms all of the time, which is entirely distinct from the speech norms of women, it is possible to see tendencies within the population which will make the choice of one type of speech appear more appropriate for one group than another. This revised view of power enables us to question competitive talk as simply powerful talk and co-operative talk as powerless. Perhaps we can see competitive talk as just as inappropriate in certain contexts as co-operative talk is in other contexts.

DISCOURSES IN CONFLICT

One final way in which feminist theorists have attempted to modify Foucault's model of discourse for feminist ends has been in analysing discourses in conflictual relations rather than in isolation. For example, in my own work, I have attempted to set discourses of femininity in relation to discourses of feminism and discourses of colonialism in the nineteenth century (Mills, 1991). For many women writers in this period, their texts were produced in the conflict of these discourses. Thus, women travel writers felt the need to include certain details in their text about their 'proper' feminine behaviour, because of their perception that only by doing so would they ensure that their audience considered them respectable. However, at the same time, these women writers also felt the pressure exerted by feminist discourses, which forced them to include mention of their position on a number of issues – thus, texts which were ostensibly travel texts made frequent allusion to the writer's political beliefs on the role of women, the correct dress for women, the oppression of women in other countries, and so on. In this sense, the discourses of feminism in the nineteenth century made it necessary for women writers to make their position on a wide range of issues clear, even when they were supposedly writing about other subjects. Similarly, discourses of colonialism/imperialism also exerted a pressure on women writers, since their position in relation to a range of issues had to be made explicit. In this sense, texts are not determined by one discourse alone (note how we often get this sense in discussions of ideology); there may be several different discourses at work in the construction of a particular text, and these discourses are often in conflict with one another. I have argued that women travel writers were caught at the conjunction of several opposing discourses and that this resulted in texts which are far from cohesive and which are fractured by these disjunctions. For example, if we consider Alexandra David-Neel's travel writing about her expedition to Tibet in the early twentieth century, her texts are caught between an impulse to present herself as an adventure–hero figure such as Richard Burton and T.E. Lawrence, and the knowledge that, because of the discourses circulating within her society about femininity, she as a woman would be considered too weak to undergo the hardships which she describes. She states: 'I would find the pass; it was my duty. I knew I would! There was no time for useless emotion' (David-Neel, 1927: 129). David-Neel is forced constantly to include details of physical difficulties and obstacles in her text, only to present herself overcoming those difficulties: 'For nineteen hours we had been walking, without having stopped or refreshed ourselves in any way. Strangely enough, I did not feel tired, only sleepy' (ibid.: 131). This phrase 'strangely enough' represents David-Neel's recognition of the strength of the discourses of feminine behaviour against which this text is being written. In order to counter these discursive pressures, she has thus to present herself as an exceptional woman who has transcended the norms for her sex, and this creates extreme tensions within the text. It is perhaps indicative of the strength of the discourses of femininity that David-Neel was accused of having lied about her journey and was forced to publish documentary evidence of her presence in Tibet. It was not thought possible, within the constraints of the discourses of femininity, that a woman could have endured what David-Neel claimed she had.

There are discursive conflicts for male writers within the colonial period, but they are of a different type, since generally the subject positions mapped out for colonial subjects are male (the adventure–hero, the upholder of civilisation, the English gentleman). Thus, we could expect greater cohesiveness in texts written by males within this period, since the subject positions mapped out for males are ones which are sanctioned and which accrue power to them. Even here, writers negotiate with these discursive constraints in conflictual relations with other discourses; for example, Joseph Conrad, in his novel *Heart of Darkness* does not simply present a conservative establishment view of colonialism. His account contains within it certain elements which seem to uphold discourses of colonialism (for example, his portrayal of Africans as essentially inarticulate and savage), whilst there are also other elements which are highly critical of colonialism, which seem to emanate from a discourse of civil liberties and human rights (for example, his depiction of the activities of the colonisers as corrupt). *Heart of Darkness* would thus appear to be constructed from a range of different discourses which makes it less cohesive as a text. It is thus difficult to pin down Conrad's position on the question of imperialism.

Travel texts by women, particularly within the colonial sphere, are clear examples of the way that discourses clash and bring about texts which seem not to be cohesive. But there are many other examples of this lack of cohesiveness which can be cited; they are generally ones where there is discontinuity, where there is change taking place. Consider, for example, a great number of advertisements at present which appear to take on board feminist phrases in order to target groups of young women consumers, but which at the same time are also signalling messages from discourses which are pre-eminently conservative and sexist. Thus, an advertisement for a perfume may portray a woman as being in control of her life, as physically fit, as pursuing a career (in short, gesturing towards feminism) whilst, at the same time, casting the perfume as a means to initiate or enrich a relationship with a male. This clash of discourses is not one which all individuals will notice since it becomes naturalised; but it becomes very marked in discourses which are in the process of change (Mills, 1995a).

CONCLUSIONS

It might be argued that it is not in feminists' interests to use the notion of discourse, since feminism as a whole is concerned with questions of subjectivity and subjection, and within discourse theory both of these terms are very difficult to use without modification. Subjection is a complex matter within discourse theory since it is less clear whether the position of those who are cast in powerless roles is simply that of victim. Since the question of agency is a vexed one within discourse theory, as I have discussed above, and the notion of our position as individual subjects is also one which it is difficult to describe, many people have turned to psychoanalytic rather than discourse theory for a model of subjectivity. Indeed, some theorists, such as McClintock, have attempted to marry the two (McClintock, 1995). However, whilst there is a less clear focus on the subject within discourse theory, perhaps for feminist theory that is welcome. Whilst within the 1960s and 1970s the notion of 'the female self' and the focus on the difference of female subjectivity was important, it has become clear that this self is produced at the expense of other less visible selves. Thus, the groundbreaking work of Judith Butler and Diana

Fuss and Queer Theory in general has been instrumental in calling into question the 'self' which Western feminism produced (Butler, 1990; Fuss; 1990). But destabilising the self is not the same as dispensing with the notion of the self, and theorists such as Butler have been quick to point out that the decentred self is still a subject. In many articles Foucault calls the self into question and proclaims the 'death of man [*sic*]', since he is attempting to write history without the subject (that is, without the liberal humanist notion of a stable, cohesive ego). Rather than focusing on the self as a fragmented and unstable amalgam of the unconscious and the conscious, Foucault sees the self as an effect of discursive structures – an effect that nevertheless interacts with those structures, but which is not foundational in itself. This more unstable notion of the self is one which has been exceptionally productive for current feminist theory, in that it does not privilege one form of homogeneous self for a group, and neither does it assume that the subject positions which can be adopted by a particular group are adopted uniformly even by members of that specific group. This form of feminist theorising is very aware that the adoption of certain subject positions is a type of action which has consequences, and it is this setting of subject positions within particular contexts of actions which feminist discourse theory makes possible (Mills and Pearce, 1996).

Feminist theory has thus significantly modified the notion of discourse by setting it more clearly in its social context and by examining the possibilities of negotiating with these discursive structures. Using the notion of discourse has made the task of constructing political agendas and courses of action far more difficult, but it has enabled feminists to construct scenarios for social change and subject positions for active women as agents.

NOTES

1 However, there are always residual traces of these earlier practices within current discourses on law and order; whilst perhaps the

reforming discourse has been dominant within the prison service since the nineteenth century, there are often calls, when right-wing governments are in power, for a more visible display of punishment for those who have been convicted of crimes – for example, the short sharp shock regime instituted under the Conservative government in the 1980s.

2 We could complicate this still further by seeing that the writer accrues a certain amount of power to herself because of her position within the non-conformist sect to which she belonged. She has aligned herself with these particular religious discourses in writing this diary, and these sects accrued power to themselves through their role within society as oppositional and subversive (Hobby, 1988).

3 Although within ideological analysis the concept of hegemony is used to describe the process whereby individuals act in ways which are not in their own interests and thus in a sense bring about their own oppression, discourse theorists would argue that this still entails a wholly negative view of the way that individuals react against and work within ideologies to construct their own sense of self. Feminist discourse theorists are concerned largely with the benefits that engaging with certain discursive structures brings to women.

4 This is a simplification of the position of feminist ideological theorists, in order to make the difference between discourse theorists and Marxist critics clear. However, it is evident that many Marxist and Marxist feminist critics see ideology as fractured and riven with contradictions, rather than simply imposed in this way (Belsey, 1980; Hennessy, 1993; Landry and MacLean, 1993). Thus, there are possibilities within ideological criticism for subjects to 'latch on' to some of these contradictions, in order to formulate a position of resistance and critique.

5

COLONIAL AND POST-COLONIAL DISCOURSE THEORY

In the previous chapter on feminist theory, I demonstrated the ways in which discourse theory can be used with a strongly political focus. A further area where this is possible is colonial and post-colonial discourse theory – the critical study of, respectively, those literary and non-literary writings which were produced within the period and context of British imperialism, and the effect of colonialism and colonial texts on current societies.[1] An extensive body of theoretical work has been developed, mainly building upon the work of Edward Said (1978, 1993), who attempted to fuse Foucauldian discourse theory with insights from Antonio Gramsci's political writings. Some of the work by theorists such as Peter Hulme (1986) and Mary Louise Pratt (1985, 1992) is detailed in this chapter to exemplify the use of the term discourse and to show the ways in which discourse has been modified. In general, this work is described as colonial discourse theory. That work which tries to question some of the assumptions of Said's work on discourse and representation, which is largely informed by psychoanalytical theory rather than discourse theory, and which is more concerned with the effects the colonial enterprise has had on current social structures and discursive formations, is known as post-colonial discourse theory, and is best exemplified by the work of Homi Bhabha (1994a) and Gayatri Chakravorty Spivak (1988, 1990, 1993b). In this chapter, I describe colonial discourse theory, since it is here that Foucault's formulation of discourse is most clearly drawn on; post-colonial theory will be drawn on principally in order to critique some of the preconceptions of colonial discourse theory, to arrive at a more complex notion of discourse. As in Chapter 4, an attempt is made to show ways in which discourse can be used productively to analyse texts, particularly in this area where the notion of discourse has arguably been most refined in recent years.

OTHERING

As I showed in Chapter 3, Foucault has provided us with a vocabulary for describing the surface regularities which can be traced across a range of texts occurring within a certain context. This is particularly useful when we consider texts written about those countries which were colonised or which suffered a form of imperial relation. Edward Said has shown that there are a number of features which occur again and again in texts about colonised countries and that these cannot be attributed simply to the individual author's beliefs, but are rather due to larger-scale belief systems structured by discursive frameworks, and are given credibility and force by the power relations found in imperialism. Peter Hulme describes colonial discourse as:

> an ensemble of linguistically-based practices unified in their common deployment in the management of colonial relation-ships ... Underlying the idea of colonial discourse ... is the presumption that during the colonial period large parts of

the non-European world were *produced* for Europe through a discourse that imbricated sets of questions and assumptions, methods of procedure and analysis, and kinds of writing and imagery.

(Hulme, 1986: 2; emphasis in original)

Colonial discourse does not therefore simply refer to a body of texts with similar subject-matter, but rather refers to a set of practices and rules which produced those texts and the methodological organisation of the thinking underlying those texts. In *Orientalism* (1978), Said described the discursive features of that body of knowledge which was produced in the nineteenth century by learned scholars, travel writers, poets and novelists, which effectively produced the Orient as a repository of Western knowledge, rather than as a society and culture functioning on its own terms. The Orient was produced in relation to the West and was described in terms of the way it differed from the West. Said argues that these colonised countries were described in ways which denigrated them, which produced them as a negative image, an Other, in order to produce a positive, civilised image of British society. These representations were structured largely according to certain discursive formats which developed over time, but which accrued truth-value to themselves through usage and familiarity. Each new text which was written about the Orient reinforced particular stereotypical images and ways of thinking. As Said argues:

Everyone who writes about the Orient must locate himself [*sic*] *vis-à-vis* the Orient, translated into his text; this location includes the kind of narrative voice he adopts, the type of structure he builds, the kind of images, themes, motifs that circulate in his text – all of which adds up to deliberate ways of addressing the reader, containing the Orient and finally representing it or speaking in its behalf.

(Said, 1978: 20)

This struggle over representation had far-reaching effects, in that it informed racist knowledge and practices, constructing the grounds within which debates about race were largely conducted and the typologies within which indigenous people and their descendants were forced to be categorised and to categorise themselves (Young, 1995). These seemingly linguistic and textual decisions about racial grouping had far-reaching material consequences which affected the rights and lives of indigenous peoples, resulting in certain groups of people being denied human status, others being used as slave labour, and still others being hunted and killed like animals (see Morris, 1979a, 1979b, 1979c; Gilroy, 1987 for an overview). These representations also determined in large measure which countries were seen to be 'open' to colonial expansion, and in need of the 'civilising' influence of the European powers (Pratt, 1992). I will now describe the discursive structures which Said has identified as constituting imperial knowledge, in order to delineate the ways in which his definition of discourse has modified Foucault's discursive model.[2]

Said does not simply focus on the jingoistic, openly propagandist texts which circulated within the colonial period; he also analyses the texts which were produced in the name of scholarship: linguistic and philological analyses, history and ethnography, together with travel writings. Pratt argues that those countries which had been colonised were reduced to being seen as objects of knowledge. Their reality was not represented as being of the same order as a Western European reality; instead, the task of colonisers, when they wrote accounts of colonised countries, was to:

> produce what they themselves referred to as 'information'. Their task . . . was to incorporate a particular reality into a series of interlocking information orders – aesthetic, geographic, mineralogical, botanical, agricultural, economic, ethnographic and so on.
>
> (Pratt, 1992: 125)

Said argues that discursive structures circulating within the nineteenth century in particular informed the way that knowledge was
produced, so that seemingly 'objective' statements were, in fact,
produced within a context of evaluation and denigration. Value-
laden statements about the inhabitants of colonised countries
were presented as 'facts' against which there was little possibility
of argument. Once this process begins, even anecdotal or fictitious
information begins to accrue to itself factual status because of
its production within the colonial nexus of power relations
(Richards, 1993; Mills, 1994b). For Said, the colonised people are
dehumanised by the series of generalisations made about them
within colonial texts. The fact that sweeping generalisations
were made about particular cultures made them less communities
of individuals than an indistinguishable mass, about whom one
could amass 'knowledge' or which could be stereotyped: the
inscrutable Chinese, the untrustworthy Arab, the docile Hindu,
and so on. Consider this example from Dr William Baikie's
Narrative of an Exploring Voyage up the Rivers Kwora and Binue
(1856), where a description of a group of people encountered on
a journey is produced as objective knowledge. However, rather
than simply describing the group, the passage has the effect of
representing them as an undifferentiated mass, and judging them
to be anomalous in relation to a Western norm:

> About half-past ten we entered a creek on the north side,
> running nearly parallel with the river, and shortly afterwards
> sighted a village, at which we soon arrived. To our astonish-
> ment the first thing which brought us up was our running the
> bow of the gig against a hut, and on looking around we found
> the whole place to be flooded. We advanced right into the
> middle of the village, and found no resting-place; right and left,
> before and behind, all was water. People came out of the huts
> to gaze at the apparition, and standing at the doors of their
> abodes were, without the smallest exaggeration, immersed

nearly to their knees, and one child in particular I observed up to its waist. How the interiors of the huts of these amphibious creatures were constructed I cannot conjecture, but we saw dwellings from which, if inhabited, the natives must have dived like beavers to get outside. We pulled in speechless amazement through this city of waters, wondering greatly that human beings could exist under such conditions . . . never had we even dreamt of such a spectacle as that of creatures endowed like ourselves, living by choice like a colony of beavers, or after the fashion of hippopotami and crocodiles of the neighbouring swamps.

(cited in Hanbury-Tenison, 1993)

This account stresses the homogeneity of the group – they are all 'creatures' and likened to animals, such as beavers, crocodiles and hippopotami. Their human characteristics are not stressed and no attempt is made to differentiate them one from the other. Not only are they characterised as belonging to a subhuman group, but it is assumed that all members of the group have always lived in this way; they are denied a history and the possibility of change. It does not strike Baikie to enquire whether these conditions are exceptional, because of a flood, or whether this is how the group of people normally live. Furthermore, they are described simply as anomalous in relation to a Western norm, as an exotic 'spectacle', as the source of 'speechless amazement', rather than as (even) the object of scientific or anthropological enquiry. Because of lack of knowledge about the group (the account is produced largely from conjecture, from a very brief encounter where no dialogue takes place), Baikie produces a description which under other circumstances would not have counted as knowledge or as factual; but, because of the institutional status of imperialism and travellers within the imperial context, his account is credited as being objective and as part of imperial knowledge. Rather than simply being an anecdote, it is authorised as part of a larger accretive knowledge system which characterised colonised nations as inferior and as subhuman.

The colonised culture was also differentiated from the colonising culture through being represented as existing on a different time-scale to the colonisers. For, as Johannes Fabian has demonstrated, colonisers set the colonised country and its inhabitants in the distant past tense, relegating them to a period which has been superseded by the colonisers, and hence denying them 'co-evalness' (Fabian, 1983). Fabian states that 'there is no knowledge of the Other which is not also a temporal, historical, a political act' (ibid.: 1). Through the use of terms such as 'backward', 'primitive', 'feudal', 'medieval', 'developing country' and 'pre-industrial' to describe colonised countries, Fabian argues, the colonised country is set within a past period of British historical development or Western progress and is therefore not permitted to exist on its own terms; it exists only in an underdeveloped parody of British civilisation, a state which Homi Bhabha has described as being one of 'mimicry' (see Bhabha, 1994b). Take, for example, this extract from a recent advertisement feature in a Sunday magazine supplement by Gavin Bate on Nepal, where he describes at some length his visit to Kathmandu:

> Kathmandu . . . resembles Tudor England with its dirty narrow streets and stout poles erected between the houses to prevent them toppling in on one another. The markets are an experience of sound and colour, every sense being invaded by the sheer spectacle of it all. A butcher squats in front of the skinned carcass of a dog, weighing gross lumps of meat on ancient scales. An elephant is led through the square laden with baskets of scarlet chillies, while brown urchins dart about with laughing faces and no clothes. Yes, Nepal is too different for anyone to prevail their own morals on what they see.
>
> (Bate, 1992: 15)

Here, Kathmandu is explicitly located as being at an arrested stage of development; it has not progressed beyond the Tudor era. It is described in terms which are very similar to the way in which Tudor England is popularly described – in terms of dirt, squalor, grossness and spectacle. Yet, this representation of Nepal located in the distant past has the effect of rendering the inhabitants of Kathmandu mere ciphers who are not taking part in the 'real-time' world of Western culture. The description of the 'laughing urchins' is particularly telling, since 'urchin' is a word which is commonly used only to describe past representations of children, and generally very uncivilised children. In this description, Bate is forced to construct Nepal (which has had an entirely different social and economic developmental history to Western Europe) into a grid of Western history and values – a process which can only result in Nepal being viewed as deficient.[3]

This setting of the other country at a different time may be explicit, as in the example above, but it may also be implicit. If we examine the above extract from Baikie again, it is clear that although the inhabitants are described as 'human' and as 'people', they are placed on a time-scale which is different from that of the narrator; by being located within the sphere of animals, they are being categorised as having achieved only a limited degree of progress on the evolutionary scale. In this way, inhabitants of colonised countries are distanced from the colonisers and British superiority is implicitly asserted.

At the same time as setting the colonised country in the distant past, colonial texts have tended to use a particular tense which Fabian terms the 'ethnographic present'; he observes that 'the present tense is a signal identifying a discourse as an observer's language' (Fabian, 1983: ix). If we examine another extract from Bate's article on Nepal, we can clearly see the effect that this use of the present tense has:

> The next day I witnessed the public stoning of a politician . . .
> The barbarism was shocking, yet in these places there is very

little grey area: affairs are very much black and white. Death, for instance is regarded simply as a transition to the next world, a station along a tram journey if you like; and the dead are burned in order to release the soul. I watched such a ceremony from start to finish: the ritualistic dipping of the body into the river, the moment when a burning torch of straw is thrust into the open mouth of the corpse and the body finally set ablaze.

(Bate, 1992: 15)

In this extract, the narrator reserves the use of the simple past tense for his own actions ('I witnessed', 'I watched') and thus sets himself firmly in time and place; he uses the incidents he witnessed to then make generalisations about the culture as a whole and its beliefs, which he assumes everyone adheres to. Statements are made about the beliefs of the culture about death ('death is regarded', 'the dead are burned', 'a burning torch is thrust', and so on) which represent the event which Bate saw as being simply an instance of a 'fact' about that culture. As Fabian puts it:

at the very least, the present tense 'freezes' a society at the time of observation; at worst, it contains assumptions about the repetitiveness, predictability and conservatism of primitives . . . (the present tense) reveals a cognitive stance towards its object . . . it presupposes the givenness of the object of anthropology as something to be observed.

(Fabian, 1983: 81–82)

The use of this present tense has the effect of making the colonised country, and its inhabitants, into an object of knowledge, reifying it and thus again denying it the status which is thereby claimed for the narrator, as a representative of the colonising powers.

Together with this use of the present tense, Fabian and Said assert that the inhabitants of the colonised country are further homogenised through the use of the third person pronoun 'he', so that global statements about the indigenous peoples are made, as if in fact they could be reduced to one single 'specimen'. Fabian observes that:

> Pronouns and verb forms in the third person mark an Other outside the dialogue. He (she or it) is not spoken to but posited (predicated) as that which contrasts with the personness of the participants in the dialogue.
>
> (ibid.: 85)

Thus, for Said, Fabian and Pratt, the important element which binds these disparate grammatical features together is that they all serve to mark off the Other from the realms of humanity.

Said also argues that colonised countries were often described in negative terms: the indigenous people were described as idle, weak, corrupt, their buildings were dirty, their culture a decaying version of a past grandeur. This negativity is a discursive feature of writing produced within the colonial context and, as with generalisation and time-placement, constitutes the discursive structures available for writers within which to produce knowledge and factual accounts . Let us examine an early example of this type of negative portrayal, written by William Dampier in *Captain Dampier's Voyage around the Terrestrial Globe* (1697), of the inhabitants of 'New Holland':

> The inhabitants of this country are the miserablest people in the world . . . They are tall, straight-bodied and thin with long small limbs. They have great heads, round foreheads, and great brows. Their eye-lids are half-closed, to keep the flies out of their eyes . . . they have great bottle noses, pretty full lips and wide mouths . . . They are long-visaged, and of a very unpleasing aspect, have no graceful feature in their faces.
>
> (cited in Carrington 1949: 354)

The negative nature of the description is excessive; it is as if only those features which could be framed within this derogatory system of knowledge are included. This negative view of the

but it has to be faced as a necessary condition of life, until a
few generations of training shall have started the Indian servant
on a new inheritance of habit. It must never be forgotten that
at present those mistresses who aim at anything beyond keep-
ing a good table are in the minority, and that pioneering is
always arduous work.

(Steel and Gardiner, 1911: 2)

Whilst the text is clearly attempting to state that Indian servants
are lazy and therefore constant vigilance is required in order to
ensure they continue to perform their duties according to British
high standards of cleanliness, the text also demonstrates the pre-
cariousness of colonial rule. Even after several centuries of British
presence in India, the 'mistress' has only to be absent for a few days
and the servants revert to their own forms of subversive behaviour.
Thus, texts can be seen to be the nexus of a range of different
discourses; 'native' resistance can be figured within texts even when
it is directly contrary to the intentions of the author.

Peter Hulme (1986) has attempted to draw on Said's work and
discourse theory in general to theorise the complexity of colonial
discourse. Rather than assuming, as Said has, that there is only
one colonial discourse, he considers there to have been various
discourses circulating within the colonial period, not all of them
characterising the indigenous subject in negative ways. He draws
attention to stereotypes such as the 'noble savage' and the 'exotic
paradise' as examples of positive representations within colonial
discourse, and shows that certain other cultures were considered
to be 'civilised'. Rather than simply representing the other culture
as deficient in relation to a Western norm, many travellers, for
example, found that the confrontation with a different culture
made them question the seemingly self-evident superiority of
Western civilisation, and many of them found that other cultures
were less 'barbaric' than their own. Alfred Wallace, an English
naturalist travelling in the Malay archipelago in 1872, noted that

Western civilisation had failed since:

> the wealth and knowledge and culture of *the few* do not
> constitute civilization, and do not advance us towards the
> perfect social state. Our vast manufacturing system, our
> gigantic commerce, our crowded towns and cities . . . create
> and maintain an ever-increasing army, whose lot is the more
> hard to bear by contrast with the pleasures, the comfort and
> the luxury which they see everywhere around them, but which
> they never hope to enjoy; and who, in this respect, are worse
> off than the savage in the midst of his tribe.
>
> (cited in Hanbury-Tenison, 1993: 62; emphasis in original)

Thus, even though there is reference to 'the savage', the more
egalitarian cultures Wallace encountered forced him to re-evaluate
the exploitation of the working classes in Victorian Britain.

CHALLENGING OTHERING

In his analysis of the variety of discourses of imperialism, Hulme
focuses on the discourse of Oriental civilisation and the discourse
of savagery which he locates in texts about the Caribbean. At the
same time as there are accounts of cannibalism and barbaric practices, there are also positive evaluations of certain aspects of the
other culture. Hulme argues that these differences are motivated
by differences of context; those cultures which resisted colonial
incursions were described as barbaric cannibals, and the colonial
powers felt justified in their attempts to exterminate them. Those
cultures which accepted colonial rule, and perhaps collaborated
with the colonial authorities in establishing settlements, were
generally characterised as civilised and peace-loving. Hulme tries
to describe the differences within discursive structures in texts
which deal with colonised countries and those where the countries
maintained their own independent governments and yet traded
with the West. Discourses change over time and depending on the

economic and social conditions within which they are generated; thus, a text about settler life within the security of the Civil Lines in Delhi during the colonial period will differ markedly from a description of the exploration of West Africa (McClintock, 1995; Darian-Smith, Gunner and Nuttall, 1996).

This is perhaps one of the greatest criticisms which has been levelled against Said's work on discourse: that he characterised colonial discourse as a homogeneous group of texts, bearing one simple message about the colonised country. This has the disadvantages both of suggesting that 'Orientalist' knowledge is all-powerful and of erasing all resistance to discursive structures. Dennis Porter has criticised Said for assuming a continuous history of oppressive representational practices from the eighteenth century through to the present day, arguing that this leads to colonial knowledge, in one form or another, being 'not only what we have but all we can ever have' (Porter, 1982: 180). This view of discourse also assumes a certain stability of representational practices, so that rather than the moments of tension or disjuncture within colonial discourse being located, it is assumed that these texts simply represent power relations. Porter gives two examples of texts which he considered to be counter-hegemonic, that is to say, which challenge imperial knowledge about other cultures. These texts, Marco Polo's *Travels* and T.E. Lawrence's *Seven Pillars of Wisdom* should be, strictly speaking, Orientalist or colonialist in Said's terms. Porter argues that there is no unified vision of the East in these texts; writing about another culture entails a heterogeneous discourse, marked by gaps, contradictions and inconsistencies. This view of the text as troubled by undercurrents from a range of different discourses allows us to read the text as containing destabilising elements, rather than as being simply a powerful tool in the oppression of another nation. Instead of searching for a unified discourse of colonialism, we should be prepared for the fact that in examining colonial texts 'no smooth history emerges, but rather a series of frag-ments, which read speculatively, hint at a story that can never be fully recovered' (Hulme, 1986: 12). Within Said's view of colonial discourse, we get the sense that Orientalist representations are being criticised in relation to a notion of the 'truth' of these countries. What post-colonial discourse theory is concerned with is that the 'truth' of those cultures is not recoverable. We will never know what those cultures were really like; all we have is our interpretations of a set of heterogeneous texts, which had effects in the real world of the time.

Gayatri Spivak is one of the post-colonial theorists whose work has been important in challenging Said's notion of the homogeneity of colonial discourse; although she has located herself theoretically more within deconstruction and Marxist feminism, her focus on the possibility of alternative voices being recoverable within discourses which seem on the surface to be simple colonialist texts has been instrumental in forcing many critics to rethink their interpretations of colonial texts (Spivak, 1993a, 1993b, 1995; see also Mills, 1994b, 1996c). In her work on the 'subaltern' subject, that is, the non-elite colonised subject, she notes that colonial texts tend to represent only certain sectors of the 'native' population. In the case of India, it is very often the elite Brahmins who are represented, particularly when they can 'be shown to have the same intentions as (thus providing legitimation for) the codifying British' (Spivak, 1993a: 77). What interests Spivak, and other theorists who form the Subaltern Studies group, is those indigenous voices which do not form part of the 'native' elite (Guha and Spivak, 1988). She suggests that, although the elite subject might be the one whose voice most approximates to colonial notions of what the Other is, it is necessary to 'insist that the colonized subaltern subject is irretrievably heterogeneous' (Spivak, 1993a: 79). Thus, Spivak is calling for a shift of theoretical position, from a concern with the voice of the coloniser or the voice of the elite colonised subject (a focus which has paradoxically only reaffirmed the position of the West) to a concern with those whose voices are often effaced by colonialist texts. The

Subaltern Studies group analyses documents not simply to accept the dominant message at face value, which in many ways entails the analyst in a straightforward collusion with the logic of colonialism; rather, as Chakrabarty has shown in his analysis of the conditions of working-class Indians in the nineteenth century, 'ruling class documents . . . can be read both for what they say and their "silences"' (Chakrabarty, 1988). By refusing to accept the surface of discourse as representing the sum total of statements on a particular situation, it is possible to analyse discursive structures as much for what they exclude as for what they determine. As I showed in Chapter 3 on discursive structures, this is very much taking Foucault's position on exclusion to its logical extreme (see Mills, 1996b, 1996c).

Mary Louise Pratt has also moved on to a more complex theorisation of discourse, since, for her, rather than colonialist texts being seen as straightforward embodiments of colonial power, they should be seen as indicative of the effect of what she terms 'the contact zone', that is, 'social spaces where disparate cultures meet, clash and grapple with each other, often in highly asymmetrical relations of domination and subordination' (Pratt, 1992: 4). Pratt does not simply examine the way that the colonisers represented the other cultures, but instead she is more concerned with the way that, although imperial writers often tried to maintain distance and differentiation between themselves and the colonised country, in fact the lived experience of colonialism was invaded by the presence of the colonised Other.

> While the imperial metropolis tends to understand itself as determining the periphery . . . it habitually blinds itself to the ways in which the periphery determines the metropolis – beginning perhaps, with the latter's obsessive need to present its peripheries and its other continually to itself.
>
> (ibid.: 6)

And, in fact, as Neil Whitehead observes, one of the striking features of colonial writing is that the knowledge which is so central to the maintenance of colonial rule could only have been produced through interaction and dialogue with 'native' guides and interpreters (Whitehead, forthcoming). Even though the knowledge which is produced from these indigenous sources is often manipulated by the colonisers, and the aim of this knowledge is often to make clear differentiation between colonised and colonising cultures, the source of this information does have a profound effect on the type of information structures which are constructed.

A further difficulty which many post-colonial theorists have found with Said's theorisation of colonial discourse is that by making discursive structures anonymous, beyond human agency, it is almost impossible to blame any individual agent for their part in imperialism. A politicised analysis of colonialism is therefore impossible. Whilst it is clear that individuals cannot be held responsible for the larger-scale organisation of imperialism, it is also clear that individuals differed in the degrees to which they championed, acquiesced or challenged imperialism. Some presented representations which destabilised British colonial involvement, whilst others affirmed colonial rule in their writings. Bernard Porter shows that many writers were openly critical of colonial intervention, and in my analyses of female travel writers it is clear that critique of colonialism and specific colonial practices is just as evident as affirmation of colonial rule (Porter, 1968; Mills, 1991). Whilst Foucault's work is important in that it allows us to focus on the way that larger-scale discursive frameworks played a role in colonial activity, it is clear that it is necessary to be able to reinscribe individual agency at some level, as I showed in Chapter 4 on feminist theory. Dennis Porter argues that the failure to take into account resistance to Orientalism by colonialists

> not only opens Said to the charge of promoting Occidentalism, it also contributes to the perpetuation of that Orientalist

thought he set out to demystify in the first place. . . . Even when he praises an occasional scholar for a rare objectivity, he does not show how, within the given hegemonic formation such an alternative discourse was able to emerge.

(Porter, 1982: 181)

PSYCHOANALYSIS AND DISCOURSE THEORY

Within the study of colonial discourse, there has developed a split between those theorists who have drawn on discourse theory and those who have turned to psychoanalysis as a framework, and the two schools of thought have differed fundamentally on their theorising of agency. Post-colonial critics such as Robert Young (1995), Homi Bhabha (1994a) and Anne McClintock (1995) have used psychoanalytic theory to describe the process of 'Othering' of colonised nations; they have described colonialism as a form of pathological disorder at a State level. The relations between the colonising State and the indigenous inhabitants are seen as characterised by paranoia: intense desire on one hand and intense fear on the other. The colonised country is invested with sexuality and becomes the object of sexual fetishism and exoticism; but at the same time, it is also the repository of irrational fears. If we consider reports of the 1857 Mutiny/Uprising in India, it is clear that the events in which women and children were killed by insurgents were reacted to by the British military and government in ways which can only be described as pathological; whilst it is clear that hundreds of British men, women and children were killed, endless stories circulated about the nature of their deaths which derived from fantasy rather than actuality. Babies were reported to have been ripped from their mother's wombs or tossed onto bayonets. Women were said to have been subjected to brutal torture and rape. The British reaction to these events was to massacre thousands upon thousands of Indians, whether connected to the uprising or not, in the most barbaric ways imaginable – firing them from cannons, forcing them to abase themselves before killing them, and so on (Sharpe, 1993).

Whilst it is occasionally useful to be able to describe the pathological behaviour of individual agents of the government, it is debatable whether the pathologising of a nation-state is theoretically productive. The attributing of the individual facets of ego-development to a nation or a government can mask the agency of individual participants in colonialism. Thus, if we attribute certain actions of Britain in the colonial period as being due to a rather ill-defined 'desire', we may be led to ignore or mask the sense in which those actions were determined by very clearly defined material, economic and social factors. It is clear that fantasy played a major role in the representing of other countries within the colonial period, but it seems necessary to develop a form of theorising which does not describe this process simply in terms of psychoanalytic concepts more suited to the description of individual psyches.

Homi Bhabha's work on mimicry and ambivalence can prove useful in the theorising of discourse, even though he locates himself fundamentally within psychoanalytic theorising (Bhabha, 1994a). His work has been used by other theorists to try to map out the discursive structures which have developed under colonialism within specific historical contexts, and this work as a whole has served to question some of the assumptions about discourse (Low, 1996). Bhabha has stressed that, despite seeming to represent the Other solely in relation to a Western norm and therefore finding the Other lacking in relation to this norm, this strategy in fact exposes an ambivalence at the very heart of colonialism, which he concludes is due to the ambivalence inherent in mimicry:

> colonial mimicry is the desire for a reformed recognizable Other, as a subject of a difference that is almost the same, but not quite. Which is to say, that the discourse of mimicry is

constructed around an ambivalence; in order to be effective, mimicry must continually produce its slippage, its excess, its difference. . . . Mimicry is thus the sign of a double articulation; a complex strategy of reform, regulation and discipline, which 'appropriates' the Other as it visualizes power. Mimicry is also the sign of the inappropriate, however, a difference or recalcitrance which coheres the dominant strategic function of colonial power, intensifies surveillance, and poses an immanent threat to both 'normalized' knowledges and disciplinary powers.

(Bhabha, 1994b: 86)

Presenting the Other as a lacking Self is here theorised as a form of complex desire on the part of the coloniser, rather than simply as an act of oppression and appropriation. The coloniser here is just as much at the mercy of these forms of representation as the colonised, and is simply caught in the play of desire and fantasy which the colonial context produces.

Anne McClintock (1995) has tried to address some of the criticisms which have been levelled against such psychoanalytic theorising, and has attempted to develop a form of theorising which is more able to deal with the specificity of colonial contexts; however, she herself analyses representations in broadly psychoanalytic terms (see also, Darian-Smith, Gunner and Nuttall 1996). Take, for example, her analysis of a treasure map in Rider Haggard's novel *King Solomon's Mines* (1881). She considers that the map in fact resembles a female body; there is a

triangle of three hills covered in 'dark heather'. This dark triangle both points to and conceals the entrances to two forbidden passages: the 'mouth of treasure cave' – the vaginal entrance into which men are led by the black mother, Gogool – and, behind it, the anal pit from which the men will eventually crawl with the diamonds, in a male birthing ritual that leaves the black mother, Gogool, lying dead within.

(McClintock, 1995: 3)

Whilst this type of analysis may seem to hold some advantages over a more literal Saidian reading, since the text is not taken at its literal meaning, but rather it is interpreted in terms of fantasy and desire, nevertheless, this type of psychoanalytic analysis of colonial texts and the process whereby one nation subjugates another in terms of sexuality, desire and fantasy does not seem productive. A discourse theorist would be interested that sexual metaphors were used to describe landscape features, but such a theorist might also remark that perhaps these features are ones which become more noticeable once one draws upon psycho-analysis when examining texts. What a discourse theorist would be interested in would be the fact that the power relations implicit within sexual relations at the time were used as a form of metaphor to describe other types of power relations. Figuring colonial relations through the analogy of the development of the individual psyche, as psychoanalytic analysis does, simply ratifies colonial expansion, seeing it as a 'natural' part of the subject's construction of its sense of self. The political agendas and power relations of nation-states are therefore erased.

Let us consider a textual example which might help us to demarcate the differences in the view of discourse as used by colonial discourse theorists such as Said, Pratt and Hulme and the views put forward by post-colonial theorists such as Bhabha and McClintock, who have used psychoanalytic theorising. Here is the final passage in E. M. Forster's *A Passage to India* (1924) where Fielding and Aziz go riding together:

> "India a nation! What an apotheosis! Last comer to the drab nineteenth century sisterhood! Waddling in at this hour of the world to take her seat! She, whose only peer was the Holy Roman Empire, she shall rank with Guatemala and Belgium perhaps!" Fielding mocked again. And Aziz in an awful rage danced this way and that, not knowing what to do, and he cried: "Down with the English anyhow. That's certain. Clear out you

fellows, double quick I say. We may hate one another, but we hate you most. If I don't make you go, Ahmed will, Karim will, if it's fifty and five hundred years we shall be rid of you, yes, we shall drive every blasted Englishman into the sea, and then," he rode against him furiously – "and then", he concluded, half kissing him, "you and I shall be friends".

"Why can't we be friends now ?" said the other, holding him affectionately. "It's what I want. It's what you want".

But the horses didn't want it – they swerved apart – the earth didn't want it, sending up rocks through which the riders must pass single-file; the temples, the tank, the jail, the palace, the birds, the carrion, the Guest House, that came into view as they issued from the gap and saw Mau beneath: they didn't want it, they said in their hundred voices, "No, not yet", and the sky said, "No, not there".

(Forster, 1924: 316)

Many critics who have drawn on psychoanalysis to analyse colonial discourse have focused on desire and the intense sexual relationships which are figured within colonial texts. Here the relation between England and India, figured through the characters of Aziz and Fielding, is seen to be one of homosexual desire, which is thwarted by seeming external factors – the sky, the horses, all of the landscape are working against this desire (Bakshi, 1994; Mills, 1994c). A psychoanalytical reading of this passage would see this process of thwarting as being one of repression and displacement of the constraint on homosexual desire. In fact, the book itself could be read as a displacement of this desire between men onto the bodies of women: the incident whereby Adela Quested is sexually 'attacked' in the caves could be read as a displacement of male homosexual desire, the process of displacement resulting in the indeterminacy of the event itself. However, a discourse theory view of this passage would be less comfortable with simply seeing these representations as one of desire. In order to read the passage as being about desire, it is necessary to foreground those elements which clearly refer to desire and minimise those which refer to other features. Thus, the elements within the passage which describe the implacable opposition of Britain and India on political terms have to be ignored; Fielding's mocking of Aziz and Indian nationalism equally has to be ignored in this presentation of the scene, as does Aziz's determination that Indians will over-throw colonial rule. A discourse theory analysis would be more concerned with the fact that questions of sexuality are seen to be central to colonial rule; as I mentioned above, this view of colonial texts would see the power relations entailed in sexual relations being used analogically for other power relations. In a sense, a discourse theory perspective would take more of a position of meta-commentary. It would see the imbrication and, in some senses, the eliding of the political and the sexual as of importance – the process whereby sexual relations between subjects were seen to stand for relations between nations.

CONCLUSIONS

Thus, colonial discourse theory and post-colonial theory have both found the notion of discourse useful in characterising the systematic nature of representations about colonised countries. Although early work stressed the way that colonised countries were Othered by the colonial powers, and saw its task as charting the strategies used by colonisers to produce representations of indige-nous peoples as deficient in relation to a British norm, more recent writing has attempted to characterise these texts as less homo-geneous and more traversed and troubled by conflicting discourses. This has changed the definition of discourse and has altered the way that discourse is used as a term. Instead of referring to a group of statements or modes of knowing, discourse is now characterised as being open to different interpretations and thus open to resistance, even when at its most seemingly powerful. Thus, within current analyses of discourse, it is no longer assumed that the dominant meaning of the discourse is the only meaning that is available within the text; instead, the knowledges which are excluded by the colonial discourses are just as important as those which are figured within the text. Thus, colonial discourse theory and post-colonial theory have troubled Edward Said's homogenising views of colonial texts, so that it is possible to characterise the relations of power between the colonised and the coloniser not simply in terms of master and slave, and not simply in terms of their success in affirming colonial power. Instead, the involvement of indigenous people in the production of colonial knowledge and in colonial resistance is now acknowledged, and a more politically productive model of discourse has been developed.

NOTES

1 Colonialism is generally used to refer to a situation where the representatives of one country invade and settle in another country, and impose a legal system, a government and other institutional structures; imperialism is the more general term which is used to signify other exploitative relations, such as when there are enforced trading relations, the imposition of an alien religion, interference with the legal system or government by a foreign body, and so on, but when there is no large-scale, planned settlement by civilians. However, since there is great variety in imperial and colonial relations (over time and within a particular context), there is not a clear-cut distinction to be made between imperialism and colonialism. The study of colonial discourse does not generally make a distinction between these relations, and I shall be using the term colonial discourse to refer to texts which are about imperial and colonial contexts. One of the differences which should perhaps be more clearly articulated is the difference between white settler cultures, such as Canada, South Africa and Australia, and non-white colonised countries, such as India and parts of Africa (McClintock, 1995). Post-colonialism is an equally problematic term, but it is generally taken to refer to the socio-economic and cultural crises caused by colonialism, amongst other factors (see Ashcroft, Griffiths and Tiffin, 1989; McClintock, 1995 for two conflicting views of the term).

2   In *Orientalism*, Said is mainly concerned with the construction of knowledge about the Orient in the nineteenth century. However, his work has been extended by other critics to other contexts, such as Africa and India (see Williams and Chrisman, 1993 for an overview of these critics). Inevitably, such extension has created difficulties for the theoretical framework within which Said was working and it has been greatly modified to deal with these new contexts (see McClintock, 1995 for an example of a theorist attempting to engage with some of these difficulties of context).

3   It could certainly be argued that there is some difficulty in using this text for analysis, since Britain does not have a colonial relation with Nepal. Said argued that the discursive structures of colonialism in fact inform the way that current societies are described.

6

DISCOURSE ANALYSIS, CRITICAL LINGUISTICS AND SOCIAL PSYCHOLOGY

Within those areas of study which draw on linguistics as a method of analysis, the term discourse is often used in ways which contrast sharply with definitions used by cultural and literary theorists. I examine three groups of theorists in this chapter, each of whom defines discourse slightly differently: discourse analysts, social psychologists and, finally, critical linguists. Each of these fields of study has approached the question of how to analyse communicative acts in context, using a form of analysis which is rigorous and based on scientific principles. Each of the fields of study is also concerned with how to analyse text in its broadest terms, which although it has been a factor within cultural/literary theory, has not been a primary concern. I deal with each of the different uses these fields have made of the term discourse briefly here, before going on to a more detailed examination of them in turn.

Within linguistics, particularly within discourse analysis, discourse is used to describe a structure which extends beyond the boundaries of the sentence. Using the analogy of sentence structure and its internal constituents (such as subject, verb, object, or noun, verb, complement), there is an assumption that elements above the level of the sentence contain similar structures. This use of the term has gained wide currency within linguistics and is used by those who would describe themselves as discourse analysts. This meaning of discourse has been developed mainly by linguists, many of them associated with English language research at Birmingham University, for example, Malcolm Coulthard, David Brazil, Martin Montgomery, Michael Hoey and Deirdre Burton, who developed a particular type of discourse analysis; that is, the analysis of the structures in spoken utterances or written text above the level of the sentence (Coulthard, 1977, 1992, 1994; Brazil, Coulthard and Johns, 1980; Burton, 1980; Coulthard and Montgomery, 1981; Hoey, 1983). These analysts have been concerned to analyse language use in context, rather than focusing on idealised abstract versions of language. I will be terming this type of work discourse analysis, to distinguish it from the discourse theory of Michel Foucault and others.[1]

Social psychologists, such as Jonathan Potter, Margaret Wetherell, Celia Kitzinger and Sue Wilkinson, have drawn upon the analytical methods developed within this type of discourse analysis and linguistics in general to develop a form of analysis which is concerned to analyse talk and particularly the structure of argument (Wetherell and Potter, 1992; Wilkinson and Kitzinger, 1995). Like discourse analysis, this approach has been concerned with structural units above the level of the sentence whilst at the same time trying to deal with the type of questions with which post-structuralist theory has engaged, most notably by focusing on such issues as power relations and the production of knowledge. As Wetherell and Potter put it:

> What post-structuralism has not done is address everyday discourse – people's talk and argument – nor has it been

concerned with materials which document interaction of one kind or another. In some ways, therefore, our general aim is to pursue post-structuralist questions with the analytic fervour of social psychologists, but in a domain of materials which have been most thoroughly explored by ethnomethodologists and conversation analysts.

(Wetherell and Potter, 1992: 89)

This type of integrated study differs from both discourse analysis and cultural theory in its use of the term discourse, in that, whilst it concerns itself with questions of power (which discourse analysis does not), it is also focused on the analysis of text, and because of its disciplinary position within social science, it is concerned with questions of data collection and analysis (which cultural theory is not necessarily). Because of this concern with methodological issues as well as wider socio-cultural factors, the definition of discourse is significantly different, since it draws elements both from Foucauldian discourse theory and more linguistics-based discourse analysis definitions. Potter and Wetherell have shown in their analysis of the discursive structures of racism that this marrying of two different views of discourse, one entailing a concern for scientific methods of analysis and the other asking larger questions of socio-cultural import, has caused great difficulty for the production of a working method of analysis which does not undermine its own claims to truth (ibid., 1992: 101).

The third definition of discourse which I examine is that of another group of linguists who use the term discourse in a slightly different way to the two previous definitions and to cultural theory as a whole. These linguists are broadly categorised as critical linguists; that is, those linguists who wish to analyse texts for political purposes. Because they argue that language is a central vehicle in the process whereby people are constituted as individuals and as social subjects, and because language and ideology are closely imbricated, the close systematic analysis of the language of texts can expose some of the workings of texts and, by extension, the way that people are oppressed within current social structures. They, like social psychologists, such as Wetherell and Potter, are largely attempting to integrate post-structuralist questions of power, truth and knowledge within their linguistic analytical methods. This group includes critical linguists such as Norman Fairclough, Tony Trew, Gunther Kress, Robert Hodge, Roger Fowler and Terry Threadgold, who have found the term discourse useful to describe structures above the level of the sentence, but who are more influenced by Michel Foucault's work and by Marxist linguistics and political theory than are the discourse analysts (Fowler *et al.*, 1979; Trew 1979a, 1979b; Hodge and Kress, 1988; Thread-gold, 1988, 1997; Fairclough, 1989, 1992a, 1992b, 1995). Their definition of discourse is more indebted to Foucault's definition, although they provide a substantial modification of the term because they are concerned with a more ground-level approach to language than Foucault; they thus provide more working models and concrete examples of how texts work to create inequalities of power, and are more concerned with the mechanics of discursive functioning. Although they share this concern with social psychologists, they tend to differ methodologically, since their frame of reference is current linguistics (rather than, as is the case with social psychologists, rather outmoded discourse analysis) and they tend thus to have adopted slightly more complex models of interpretation and meaning. Their form of analysis is usually less concerned with content-analysis or thematic analysis and more with questions of the possible meanings of different discourses used by participants in speech and in text.

As I stated at the beginning of this chapter, all of these theorists are concerned with the rigorous analysis of written text or speech, and thus their definitions of discourse differ from those of cultural and literary theorists. However, because of difference in degree in their theoretical affiliations with linguistics, social science and/ or literary and cultural theory, their definitions of discourse differ significantly, and the types of analyses which they produce vary greatly one from another.

DISCOURSE ANALYSIS

Discourse analysis can be seen as a reaction to a more traditional form of linguistics (formal, structural linguistics) which is focused on the constituent units and structure of the sentence and which does not concern itself with an analysis of language in use.[2] Discourse analysis, in contrast to formal linguistics, is concerned with translating the notion of structure from the level of the sentence, i.e., grammatical relations such as subject–verb–object, to the level of longer text. Since it is rare for anyone to communicate with others through single sentences alone, these discourse analysts are critical of the tendency for linguists to concentrate solely on sentence structure. As Michael Hoey states:

> Conversation involves an interchange between two or more people in which each contributor may produce more than one utterance and each contribution builds (normally) upon the previous contributions either directly or indirectly. We know immediately if, for example, the subject matter of a conversation changes and will comment on it appropriately if it appears to have been for ulterior motives or because of some misunderstanding. Similarly, in writing, sentences bunch into conventional units called paragraphs, paragraphs into chapters, and chapters into books. In short, in our everyday speech and writing, the sentence is only a small cog in a normally much larger machine.
>
> (Hoey, 1983: 1)

Thus, this type of discourse analysis has developed out of a desire to analyse these larger units and structures which are implicitly recognised by speakers and hearers at the level of discourse, rather than at the level of the sentence. These larger structures may be more difficult to analyse, precisely because of their largely unanalysed and taken-for-granted nature. However, conversations can be seen to be structured, and can be analysed in terms of the moves which participants make to signal that, for example, they are initiating a new topic of conversation or that they are reviving an older topic of conversation; these moves which 'chunk' speech into functional segments and which participants recognise as segmented, are signalled clearly by the use of discourse markers with phrases such as 'well', 'OK' and 'anyway'. These discourse markers only function at the level of discourse, signalling the end of an exchange or the initiation of a new topic, and they do not have a function at the level of the sentence. Thus, a marker such as 'anyway', signals clearly to participants in a conversation that a transitional moment has been reached and that a change of topic or a leave-taking is about to be introduced. It is hard to say that 'anyway' has any other meaning or function than as a discourse marker. It is these higher-level organisational features of conversation and text, and the higher-order structuring and segmenting of text, which are of interest to discourse analysts.

Discourse analysts such as Malcolm Coulthard and John Sinclair (1975) assume that there is a ranking of structures within discourse; thus, just as there is a hierarchical relation between sentences and clauses (sentences are made up of clauses), so there is a hierarchical relation between transactions, exchanges, moves and acts, with acts being the lowest unit of analysis. When Sinclair and Coulthard analysed the discourse structures within the classroom, they were interested in 'the level of the function of a particular utterance, in a particular social situation and at a particular place in a sequence, as a specific contribution to a developing discourse' (Sinclair and Coulthard, 1975: 13). They saw their task as isolating and describing the workings of a limited number of these functional units. A transaction, such as a teacher–pupil interaction, consists of exchanges, and they classified them as eliciting, directing, informing, and so on. In this sense, they were more concerned with what the participants were actually doing with words (the functional value) than with the meaning of the words or utterances. An exchange, such as an eliciting exchange, is seen to consist of smaller units, which they termed 'moves', and they classified these using terms such as initiating, response, and so on. Let us examine an example from their analysis of an interaction within a lesson:

1 *Teacher*: Can you tell me why do you eat all that food? Yes.
2 *Pupil*: To keep you strong.
3 *Teacher*: To keep you strong. Yes. To keep you strong. Why do you want to be strong?

(ibid.: 107)

Sinclair and Coulthard analyse this as part of an eliciting exchange, since its primary function is to elicit information. The exchange is made up of moves: the first utterance in line 1 by the teacher is an initiating move; the pupil then makes a responding move in line 2, and the teacher then makes a feedback move in line 3, when s/he repeats the pupil's utterance to confirm that this was the answer s/he was seeking. S/he then goes on to make another initiating move which constitutes a new exchange. Moves are described as consisting of acts, which are not necessarily coterminous with sentences, but which could be said to be composed of groups of words within an utterance/text which have a recognisable function. In line 1 the teacher says 'yes', which could be classified as a nominating act, in that the teacher clearly chooses a pupil to answer. In line 3, the same word 'yes' has a different function and could be classified as a confirming act, in that, like the repetition of the pupil's utterance by the teacher, it serves to indicate to the pupil that the answer is acceptable.[3] Fairclough states that this is one of the strengths of Sinclair and Coulthard's analysis, since 'it draws attention to systematic organizational properties of dialogue and provides ways of describing them' (Fairclough, 1992b: 15).

As well as being concerned to describe the structural units within a text or utterance, discourse analysis is concerned with language in use; rather than examples which have been invented by the linguist or which have been found in textbooks, discourse analysts are interested in 'real' naturally occurring language, usually either tape-recorded speech (for example, the interaction between a teacher and a class of students, or a dialogue between a doctor and patient), or texts such as instruction manuals, books for children, newspaper editorials, and so on, which have a communicative function and are not therefore invented for the purpose of analysis (Coulthard, 1977, 1994; Brown and Yule, 1983).[4] Take for example this extract from a conversation analysed by Brown and Yule:

A: so father was making up a big..sort of remembrance book

B: aha

A: to give him and he was writing just at the beginning he was writing.. writing the whole..for each year of his life he wrote something in that had..had been invented or..

B: oh yes

A: ah a book that had been written or a piece of music that had been written or a painting or a. . .

B: very interesting yes

A: or

whatever you know and..within his lifetime the telephone had been invented..

B: had it.. really.. fancy.

(Brown and Yule, 1983: 92; ..*represents a pause*)

This extract differs quite markedly from examples used within traditional linguistics, in that it is a transcription of a conversation, displaying all of the false starts, hesitations and incoherences of naturally occurring conversation. Brown and Yule in their analysis are not concerned with the meaning of the exchange, but rather they are interested in the functions of particular items within the larger discourse as a whole. Here they are interested in topic control, and they comment 'Speaker B stops trying to take turns in the negotiation of topic and waits for speaker A to make it clear how what she is saying has some connection to the existing topic framework' (ibid.: 92). Thus, B's utterances (which are classified as 'backchannel behaviour' – those noises which are made by someone in a conversation, such as 'hmmm', 'yes', 'mmm', but which do not interrupt the speaker) indicate to the speaker that s/he should continue to speak, and that the hearer understands what is being said. They also indicate to speaker A that speaker B is prepared to have speaker A define the topic of conversation at this point and make clear to him/her how it relates to the overall topic of talk. Once this has been established, speaker B will be able to contribute to the talk. This type of analysis, like Sinclair and Coulthard's, is interested in the function of particular items within the ongoing speech or text as whole, rather than their meaning or interpretation in isolation from one another.

As well as analysing conversations, discourse analysts have also examined written texts. Deirdre Burton has applied the types of descriptive frameworks developed for analysing exchanges in conversational interactions to dialogue in drama, and has produced a model for describing the way that certain types of modernist drama dialogue contain violations of discursive norms (Burton, 1980). Michael Hoey, and Gillian Brown and George Yule have also demonstrated the way that discourse analysis can be applied to written text (Brown and Yule, 1983; Hoey, 1983). Brown and Yule discuss the way that cohesive relations function across discourse – thus, they analyse the way that chunks of text 'stick' together. In this example, they analyse the way that information is structured in a recipe for chicken korma:

> Slice the onion finely, brown in the butter and then place in a small dish. Put the ground spices into a breakfast cup of water,

> add to the fat in the pan and cook for 3 minutes, stirring the while. Now add the chicken, mix well, see that the meat is just covered by water and boil for 20 minutes with the lid on the pan.
>
> (Brown and Yule, 1983: 175)

What interests Brown and Yule here is the way that an ideal reader makes sense of this passage, partly because of their knowledge of the structures usually found in the genre of recipes, but also partly to do with the way that readers have internalised a set of models of discourse organisation; the reader thus knows that, in the first sentence when the writer says 'brown in the butter and place in a small dish', the object which is implicitly referred to is 'the onion', and the onion which has to be placed in the small dish must have already been browned in the butter. These rules of making sense of ellipted items within a text are not usually analysed explicitly, but they perform a major role in the discourse information structures within written texts. As Brown and Yule state, in this type of textual analysis:

> Our interest does not lie simply in describing the form of the expression, which is obviously of prime interest to the sentence grammarian. Our interest lies in observing the forms in the context in which they are used. We want to know how speakers, having a given quantum of information to impart, identify and package that information.
>
> (ibid.: 176)

Thus, discourse analysis of written text aims to make explicit those implicit norms and rules for the production of language, and is particularly interested in the way that discourse consists of sets of hierarchical units which make up discursive structures.

Discourse analysis has been very important in opening up new areas of analysis: initiating the analysis of systematic organisational properties of language and attempting to develop a system of notation and description for these organisational units. However, it has been criticised for a number of reasons. Firstly, even though it considers language in use in 'real' language contexts, discourse analysis does not concern itself with questions of the way that social relations impinge upon the production of speech or written texts and on the power relations between participants, nor does it concern itself with questions of interpretation, or whose view of what the function of a particular item is taken by the analyst. Norman Fairclough has been very critical of this type of analysis, terming it 'non-critical'. Of Sinclair and Coulthard's work analysing teacher–pupil interaction he states:

> its limitations are the absence of a fully developed social orientation to discourse, and insufficient attention to interpretation. These limitations can be related to their choice of data; they concentrate on a traditional teacher-centred mode of classroom discourse, and their data does not reflect the diversity of current classroom practices. This makes classroom discourse seem more homogeneous than it actually is, and naturalises dominant practices. It presents them as simply 'there', rather than as having been put there through processes of contestation with alternative practices, and as having been 'invested' with particular ideologies (e.g. views of learners and learning), and as helping to sustain particular relations of power within society. In short, the Sinclair and Coulthard approach lacks a developed social orientation in failing to consider how relations of power have shaped discourse practices, and in failing to situate classroom discourse historically in processes of social struggle and change.
>
> (Fairclough, 1992b: 15)

The problem of interpretation is not one which concerned discourse analysis at first; the text was viewed as a simple product which could be interpreted by the analyst. What Sinclair and Coulthard failed to recognise was that their interpretation and analysis of the text was very much that of the speaker in power in the discourse situation, i.e., the teacher. More recent work in discourse analysis and in critical linguistics (most notable Fairclough's (1992b) work) has shown that utterances do not simply mean one thing and that they cannot therefore be interpreted from the standpoint of the speaker or hearer alone; there is a sense in which utterances are ambivalent and are interpreted by participants according to hypotheses and working models that they develop in the course of the conversation (Mey, 1993). This can be seen clearly in the contrast between the type of discourse analysis of doctor–patient interviews undertaken by David Brazil (1975), and the form of critical linguistic analysis carried out by Fairclough, discussed later in this chapter. Briefly, Brazil assumes that the function of particular utterances is transparent, and that the position of the analyst in allocating each act or move to a particular categorisation is one of scientific disinterestedness, whereas Fairclough assumes that each of the participants will view the functioning of utterances from a standpoint made up of different interests and preoccupations – the analyst has therefore to be careful not to elide his/her position of analysis with that of one of the participants.

Thus, discourse analysis has provided a range of tools for describing the structures and functioning of language within utterances, and it has forced many mainstream and traditional linguists to shift their attention from words in isolation to words within context. It has been highly influential in psychology and sociology as a method for analysing stretches of interaction rather than isolated phrases. Its methodology has been adopted by many analysts in different fields, but perhaps it is the methodology itself which is open to criticism more than any other aspect of the analysis; in examining the way that social psychologists have made use of discourse analysis these methodological difficulties will be made apparent.[5]

SOCIAL PSYCHOLOGISTS AND DISCOURSE

Social psychologists, as I mentioned in the introduction to this chapter, are concerned to integrate questions raised by post-structuralist theory and more broadly sociological analysis, with a methodology which is rigorous and replicable. Thus, the definition of discourse which they use tends to be largely that formulated by Foucault, but because their methodological framework is drawn from discourse analysis, where a different model of discourse is used, their own use of the term discourse vacillates rather disconcertingly from one to the other. I examine two types of discourse analysis undertaken by social psychologists, each of which aims to consider questions of power and oppression, drawing on the type of discourse analysis detailed in the previous section.

Margaret Wetherell and Jonathan Potter's *Mapping the Language of Racism* demonstrates very clearly the way that discourse analysis can aid the investigation of discourses such as racism. They have chosen the area of racism because they found Foucauldian theorising of discourse ran the risk of seeming rather abstract and separate from the lives of real people. They liken discourse theory analysis to the analysis of plate tectonics in geology:

> a patchwork of plates/discourses are understood to be grinding violently together, causing earthquakes and volcanoes, or sometimes sliding silently one underneath the other. Discourses become seen as potent causal agents in their own right, with the processes of interest being the work of one (abstract) discourse on another (abstract) discourse. . . . In contrast to this, we wish to place much more emphasis on discourse as social practice, on the context of use and thus on the act of discursive instantiation.

> (Wetherell and Potter, 1992: 90)

Rather than assuming that there is one single discourse of racism, and challenging it on a moral basis, as many analysts have done, they attempt to chart the constituent elements within a set of extracts taken from the racist utterances of a group of white (Pakeha) New Zealanders. They see racist discourse as having outcomes in the real world in that it has the effect of categorising and discriminating between certain groups, and it legitimises the practices which keep the Pakeha New Zealanders in their positions of power. They aim to separate out the argument structures within discourses of racism which cast Maoris as different and inferior to Pakehas. For example, in this interview they analyse the rhetorical work which goes into making racist statements without being heard as racist:

Wetherell: Do you think New Zealand can be described generally as a violent society ? In terms of crime rate and

Jones: Yes, it has got a very high crime rate. um. yes I think so. It's not as bad as some places though. but the crime rate is going up

Wetherell: Uhm. Why do you think, what's responsible there and what could be done about it? (pause)

Jones: To really answer that you'd have to look at. the types of crime you've got. ah. and who's committing them

Wetherell: Yes. Uhmm

Jones: There have been you know ideas put out what it is, that the majority of rapes are committed by Islanders or Maoris and a lot of house burglaries I would imagine are committed by kids and the majority of the kids that are hanging around the streets are Islanders, they're not the Maoris, well, it's unfair to say the Maoris because the Maoris

I know are quite nice really. Yes. Maoris. are quite
good. It's the Islanders that come here and can't
handle it.

(ibid.: 96)

What Wetherell and Potter find of interest in this extract is the
effort which the speaker expends to manage a dilemma – how to
express racist beliefs without being condemned. They state:

the dilemma is managed by constructing evaluations as part of
the world, as a bad thing which is simply described, rather than
an expression of personal negative attitudes to this group.

(ibid.: 97)

Thus, rather than being open about his racist attitudes, the
speaker here attributes the high crime rate to particular groups of
Maoris or Polynesian migrants (Islanders) and this is posited as
simply factual. He distances himself from this particular view in
some ways because he states that the Maoris he knows are 'quite
nice'; thus he presents himself as someone who is not prejudiced
at the same time as detailing views which are racist. Attention to
discourse here is manifested in the concern with power relations
which an analysis of racism demonstrates. Thus, Foucault's
analysis of power relations is exemplified in the types of speech
which are analysed; but this type of rhetorical and argument
analysis draws on and modifies the methodologies of discourse
analysis, in that what Wetherell and Potter are interested in is
the structures which this stretch of talk shares with other similar
interactions.

Where perhaps this type of analysis could be criticised is in its
use of a rather outmoded form of discourse analysis. Much of the
form of the analysis is content analysis, whereby an example of an
interaction is transcribed, and then parts of the conversation or
argument are glossed as belonging to certain types of structural
groupings. Thus, much of Wetherell and Potter's analysis of

racism consists of separating out the different functions and values attributed to the key terms such as 'culture' in racist discourses. Consider this example where one participant states:

> I think it's important they [Maoris] hang on to their culture because if I try to think about it, the Pakeha New Zealander hasn't got a culture. As far as I know he hasn't got one unless it's rugby, racing and beer, that would be his lot!
>
> (ibid.: 129)

Wetherell and Potter gloss this in the following terms: 'Maoris in this formulation become museum keepers. Theirs is the privilege and burden of heritage' (ibid.). Thus, discourse analysis here simply seeks to rephrase at a more general level elements of rhetorical structure which consistently appear within a discourse and which seem to define that discourse. In essence, this is simply a form of analysis of the meaning of particular key terms within racism. Thisapproach shares with discourse analysis a problematic eliding of the position of the speaker with that of the analyst, which I discussed in the previous section. Thus, in this discussion of racism, the utterances of white New Zealanders are considered to be transparent in meaning; the opinions of Maoris or Polynesian migrants are not sought and nor are their interpretations of these utterances considered.

A similar concern with questions of power relations occurs in the collection of essays edited by Sue Wilkinson and Celia Kitzinger *Feminism and Discourse* (1995). These essays attempt to use the concerns of discourse theory (here largely restricted to power relations and truth/knowledge) with the methodology of discourse analysis for feminist ends, examining such issues as sexual harassment, menstruation, anorexia and heterosexual desire. In an essay attempting a feminist post-structuralist discourse analysis of menstruation, Kathryn Matthews Lovering demonstrates how she moved from a fairly conventional psychological analysis of menstruation to a discourse view of the subject, whereby she tried to chart the way that menstruation is discursively constructed for and by young girls approaching the menarche. She is further concerned with the way that these discursive structures then map out subject positions for adolescent girls and boys. She analyses some of the answers to a question she asks some school girls about physical changes during adolescence:

A: They [school teachers] don't talk about the boys very much, only the girls.

A: It doesn't seem fair. They are laughing at us. Not much seems to happen to the boys.

A: Girls all go funny shapes.

A: Because the boys they don't really . . . change very much. They just get a little bigger.

(Lovering, 1995: 23)

From her analysis of similar statements made by a number of different girls she is able to make generalisations about the discursive positions available to them to express themselves on the question of menstruation: she comments that 'the female body has become the reproductive and sexual body, and the object of fascination and regulation . . . these constructions of the female and male body as essentially different, always already sexed, and private, regulate the knowledge that children (and adults) have of the body and the menstrual cycle' (ibid.: 23–24). Thus, the discursive construction of menstruation as a separating of male and female bodies has a profound effect, not only on the way that menstruation is viewed but on how these adolescents view their relations with males and with other females.

Analyses such as those contained in the essays on feminism and discourse are important in investigating the discursive construction of knowledge about women. However, as I mentioned in my discussion of Wetherell and Potter's work, they have not sufficiently criticised the use of discourse analysis and its compatibility with discourse theory. It is only when we turn to the work of critical linguists that such an integration seems to be more fully worked through.

CRITICAL LINGUISTS/DISCOURSE THEORISTS

Because of these difficulties in analysis, critical linguists/discourse theorists have developed a radically different form of analysis, which inflects the term discourse slightly differently. This group of linguists have been concerned to develop a political analysis of text and, particularly in the case of linguists such as Norman Fairclough, they have integrated Michel Foucault's definition of discourse with a systematic framework of analysis based on a linguistic analysis of the text (Fairclough, 1989, 1992a, 1992b, 1995; see also, Fowler *et al.*, 1979; Hodge and Kress, 1988). Early work in this area is best exemplified in the collection of essays by Fowler *et al.* entitled *Language and Control* (1979), especially Tony Trew's influential essay, where he demonstrates that small-scale linguistic choices result in particular messages for the text as a whole. For example, he analysed a series of South African newspaper headlines where the overall message of the text seemed to depend on choices over the use of the passive or active voice. Thus, one newspaper headline read:

RIOTING BLACKS SHOT DEAD BY POLICE AS ANC LEADERS MEET
(*The Times*, 1975, cited in Trew, 1979a: 94)

Trew argues that choosing the passive voice (Blacks [are] shot by police) has the effect of making the actions of the Black people more salient than the actions of the police. Furthermore, choosing to place the term 'rioting Blacks' first has the effect of minimising the actions of the police. He contrasts this with a phrase like 'Police shoot Blacks', where it is clear who is responsible for the unrest. By modifying the term 'Blacks' by the word 'rioting', Trew argues, a value judgement is implicit in the headline as to who is responsible for the unrest. Trew is concerned with the systematic choices of elements like passive rather than active voice over a stretch of text, and is thus moving towards an analysis of text which is concerned not with individual language items, but with the effect of repeated choices on the meaning and force of the text as a whole. However, this type of analysis tended to suffer from the same theoretical problems as discourse analysis; for example, viewing the text as a product, assuming that language items had a single meaning which all analysts could agree on, and so on. However, in later work, the theoretical questions which Foucault's work elicits are more fully integrated in small-scale analytical contexts; discourse as a term begins to be used in a systematic way so that the constituents of discourse can be described. As Fairclough puts it, discourse is often used by recent critical linguists to:

> refer to the different ways of structuring areas of knowledge and social practice. Thus the discourse of 'medical science' is currently the dominant one in the practice of health care, though it contrasts with various wholistic 'alternative' discourses (e.g. those of homeopathy and acupuncture) as well as popular 'folk' discourses. . . . Discourses do not just reflect or represent social entities and relations, they construct and constitute them.
>
> (Fairclough, 1992b: 3)

These linguists have therefore been concerned with inflecting Foucault's analysis of discourse with a political concern with the effects of discourse; for example, the way that people are positioned into roles through discursive structures, the way that certain peoples' knowledge is disqualified or is not taken seriously in contrast to authorised knowledge, and so on. In this way, critical linguists such as Fairclough can be seen to be providing working models and forms of practice from Foucault's theoretical interventions, together with a description of the effects of discursive structures on individuals. In contrast to 'non-critical' linguistics, critical linguistics does not just describe:

> discursive structures, but also [shows] how discourse is shaped
> by relations of power and ideologies, and the constructive
> effects discourse has upon social identities, social relations and
> systems of knowledge and belief, neither of which is normally
> apparent to discourse participants.
>
> (ibid.: 12)

It is this shift away from mere description to a more analytical and critical perspective which is a significant reinterpretation of Foucault's work through the matrix of linguistics' concern for replicable, verifiable analyses.

In order to illustrate this particular use of discourse I will focus on Norman Fairclough's work, because he is one of the few theorists who openly acknowledges his debt to Foucault and Pecheux, whilst stating clearly that his is not a simple application of their work. He argues that, because his form of critical discourse analysis developed solely in relation to the structure of spoken and written language texts, his concerns will inevitably be different to Foucault's. But why he believes that Foucault is so important to linguistics is because of his work's emphasis on the 'major role of discourse in the constitution of social subjects' (Fairclough, ibid.: 44). Linguistics has largely ignored questions of the role of language in the constitution of subjectivity and selfhood, and it is for this reason that Foucault's notion of discourse can allow for this type of analysis to be integrated into linguistic study.[6]

Fairclough argues that Foucault's work on discourse can be usefully drawn on by linguists for two main insights: '1. the constitutive nature of discourse – discourse constitutes the social, including "objects" and social subjects; 2. the primacy of inter-discursivity and intertextuality – any discursive practice is defined by its relations with others, and draws upon others in complex ways' (ibid.: 55). By this he means that he is concerned with the way that what we consider to be the social is largely constructed through the operations of discourse; and secondly he is interested in the way that there are relations between and within discourse structures. What Fairclough adds to Foucault's work is close linguistic analysis and reference to 'real' texts in context, and also this notion that discourses refer to each other and are constituted in that process of reference. He finds problematic Foucault's lack of reference to real practice by individuals and also his lack of address to the practicalities of struggle and change. I will deal with these two elements of Fairclough's work in turn. Firstly, the notion that discourse constitutes the social and thus social subjects: he focuses on the discursive construction of social relations and 'the self' within particular contexts, most notably in the medical sphere. He gives several examples of dialogues between doctor and patient, where the doctor controls the turn-taking system (who speaks, for how long, on what topic, and who comments on the foregoing speech and glosses it for its overall meaning). Fairclough demonstrates that in these interactions the patient attempts to foreground her own concerns in her medical condition, but they are ignored by the doctor who only wishes to address those elements of her condition which relate to his diagnosis. For example, a patient is describing a stomach pain that she has:

Patient: It's all right up here in the front

Doctor: And when do you get that?

Patient: Well, when I eat something wrong

Doctor: How soon after you eat it?

Patient: Well, probably an hour . . . maybe less

Doctor: About an hour?

Patient: M a y b e less . . . I've cheated and I've been drinking which I shouldn't have done

Doctor: Does drinking make it worse?

Patient: Ho ho uh ooh yes . . . especially the carbonation and the alcohol

Doctor: How much do you drink?

Patient: I don't know . . . enough
            to make me go to sleep at night . . . and that's quite a
            bit

Doctor: One or two drinks a day?

(Mishler, cited in ibid.: 139)

In this extract from the interview, one has 'the sense of the doctor shifting and constraining topic in accordance with a pre-set agenda, which the patient is not being allowed to disturb' (ibid.: 141). Fairclough is concerned with the way that the doctor focuses only on the things which he feels are relevant. Thus, the patient is clearly trying to inform the doctor that she has a number of problems, with sleeping, for example, which alcohol seems to alleviate; the doctor focuses only on the amount of alcohol and disregards the information which relates to problems of sleeping. What makes this type of analysis different to standard discourse analysis is that Fairclough is interested just as much on the failed attempts of the patient to assert her speaking rights as he is in the more successful doctor's interventions. Furthermore, Fairclough does not assume that he knows what the patient means or what motivates her. When she hesitates at certain points of the medical examination (using 'well', 'hmm') and displays a low affinity in her modal choice (i.e., showing a low degree of commitment to the probability of truth value of one of her statements; for example, when she answers, 'I don't know' to a question which she then goes on to answer) Fairclough comments:

It is difficult to disentangle factors of propositional truth and social relations in the patient's motivation for [this choice]; does she select low modality because she is not sure how accurate the gloss is, or because she is reluctant to claim anything resembling medical knowledge in an interaction with a legitimized medical expert? Propositional truth and social relations, knowledge and power, seem to be intricately linked in such cases.

(ibid.: 142)

Thus, Fairclough is not content simply to describe the constituents of the interaction, nor does he simply describe the imposition of power within a particular setting, as has been done frequently by ethnomethodologists and conversation analysts before; rather, he is more concerned with the way in which this type of interaction displays the complexity of the workings of power relations within the society as a whole. He is not solely concerned with analysing the way that the doctor asserts his control, but by focusing on the patient's often ambivalent responses and interjections, he is able to see the interaction as more fragmented and less well ordered than it at first appears. He sees the interventions of the patient and the doctor constituting different discourses which clash in this encounter: the voice of technological medicine ('a technological rationality which treats illness in terms of context-free clusters of physical symptoms') and the voice of the patient's 'lifeworld' ('a "commonsense" rationality which places illness in the context of other aspects of the patient's life') (ibid.: 144)). The discourse of technological medicine consists of a series of seemingly un-connected questions which focus only on certain aspects of the patient's life and behaviour; the discourse of the patient's lifeworld focuses on the illness which the patient has in relation to all other aspects of the patient's life. Fairclough contrasts this type of medical interview with one between a homeopath and his/her patient and is thus able to set the technological medical interview alongside a type of discourse which challenges its fundamental bases. These two types of medical discourse do not simply coexist; they are in conflict. He comments: 'In struggles between varieties of medical interview, it is boundaries within orders of discourse, such as the boundary between counselling and medical interview, and the interdiscursive articulation of elements within orders of discourse, that are at issue' (ibid.: 148). In this way, Fairclough is able to show that social relations are not simply the imposition of one discourse type or another (i.e., that of the doctor on the patient), but are rather constituted by the clash of different discourse types for ascendancy within interactions.

The second element which Fairclough focuses on – the relational nature of discourse – is dealt with particularly in his treatment of Julia Kristeva's term 'intertextuality', which, in its original usage, could be defined broadly as the propensity of texts to refer to others and to be constructed by that reference to other texts. This term is not generally employed in discussions of discourse, but here Fairclough is trying to deal with the specific constituents of discourse, rather than its abstract constitution. Fairclough modifies Kristeva's definition, setting it more within a Foucauldian framework, locating this intertextual reference within a social context and stressing the fact that intertextuality is one of the discursive mechanisms which brings about change within discourses. Fairclough links intertextuality with hegemony, that is, the manner in which individuals collude in their own oppression:

> The concept of intertextuality points to the productivity of texts, to how texts can transform prior texts and restructure existing conventions (genres, discourses) to generate new ones. But this productivity is not in practice available to people as a limitless space for textual innovation and play: it is socially limited and constrained, and conditional upon relations of power. The theory of intertextuality cannot itself account for these social limitations, so it needs to be combined with a theory of power relations and how they shape (and are shaped by) social structures and practices.
>
> (ibid.: 103)

In short, Fairclough has added Foucault's interest in power relations to Kristeva's purely textual concept in order to be able to describe some of the mechanisms whereby discourses have an effect on individuals as social subjects.

Where Fairclough differs most markedly from discourse analysts is in his concern with ambivalence. For discourse analysts such as Sinclair and Coulthard, the meaning of discourse units is clear and unambiguous; Fairclough stresses that textual meaning is sometimes indeterminate and that units within a discourse are subject to different interpretations. For him, intertextuality is one aspect of textual construction which brings about ambivalence within a text; if a statement from one text is integrated into another, it creates some sort of disjunction: 'if the surface of a text may be multiply determined by the various other texts which go into its composition, then elements of that textual surface may not be clearly placed in relation to the text's intertextual network' (ibid.: 105).

Let us consider an example which Fairclough gives of the way that intertextuality manifests itself in texts, and the way that this can be a focus for an analysis which is concerned with the way that discourse structures have an effect on power relations. He takes a report in the *Sun* newspaper in 1985 about drug dealing with the heading 'Call up forces in drug battle!' This is an extract from the article:

> The armed forces should be called up to fight off a massive invasion by drug pushers, MPs demanded yesterday. Cocaine pedlars are the greatest threat ever faced by Britain in peacetime – and could destroy the country's way of life, they said. The MPs want Ministers to consider ordering the Navy and the RAF to track down suspected drug-running ships approaching our coasts. On shore there should be intensified law enforcement by Customs, police and security services . . . In one of the hardest hitting Commons reports for years, the committee – chaired by Tory lawyer MP Sir Edward Gardiner – warned gravely: 'Western society is faced by a warlike threat from the hard-drugs industry. The traffickers amass princely incomes from the exploitation of human weakness . . . ' The Government is expected to bring in clampdown laws in the autumn.
>
> (cited in ibid.: 106)

In his analysis, Fairclough is concerned with the intertextual relation and transformation between the original document – the report from the all-party Home Affairs Committee – and the newspaper article. He notes that, in formal terms, the segments of the text which 'belong' to the *Sun* reporter, David Kemp, and those which 'belong' to the chair of the committee are clearly demarcated: Gardiner's words are placed within direct quotation marks, and MPs' words are placed in indirect speech marked by phrases such as 'MPs demanded' and 'they said'. However, by referring to the original committee document, Fairclough is able to show that the article on the whole is a blending of the voice of the *Sun* with that of the committee report, so that it is often not clear who is speaking. He takes as an example the headline: 'Call up forces in drug battle!' The headline itself is not marked by inverted commas, but because it contains an exclamation mark, a marker of speech, we are led to believe that the *Sun* is here reporting someone's words; there is thus a fundamental ambivalence as to who is speaking. Fairclough cites a section of the original report and compares it to the *Sun* article:

> The Government should consider the use of the Royal Navy and the Royal Air Force for radar, airborne and ship surveillance duties. We recommend therefore that there should be intensified law enforcement against drug traffickers by H. M. Customs, the police, the security services and possibly the armed forces.
>
> (ibid.: 110)

Fairclough shows the way in which the article transforms the original report, by translating vocabulary items and substituting words like 'pusher' for 'trafficker', but also setting the report within a metaphorical framework of war and battle, which entails the use of phrases like 'call up', 'invasion', 'fight off', and so on. In this example of intertextuality, Fairclough finds that there is ambiguity as to whose voice is being represented, and also he finds that the voice of the committee report becomes merged with the voice of the *Sun* so that the cautious recommendations which the report makes become the *Sun*'s own clearer, more polarised demands. Fairclough tracks down this tendency in newspapers to act as mediators between official bodies and the people at large, in effect translating these documents into a form which they feel more closely approximates the language usage of their intended readers. In this process they effect:

> the ideological work of transmitting the voices of power in a disguised and covert form. Translating the language of official written documents into a version of popular speech is one instance of a more general translation of public language . . . into private language: a linguistic shift which is itself part of the rearticulating of the relationship between the public domain of the political (economic, religious) events and social agents, and the private domain, the domain of the 'lifeworld', of common experience.
>
> (ibid.: 110)

In this type of analysis, Fairclough is thus able to connect very careful, detailed, close textual analysis with discourse processes occurring within the larger social community and larger social changes affecting the relationship between the public and private domains. Thus, whilst there have been innumerable linguistic analyses of texts which have been informed by political concerns, Fairclough is one of the few analysts who have attempted to map out the connection between a close textual analysis and wider discourse structures.

CONCLUSIONS

Within this chapter I have tried to distinguish between those linguists who use discourse to mean the analysis of the structures of a piece of extended text, an analysis which will focus on the higher-level organisation of that piece of text, and those linguists and social psychologists who have used Foucault's work to develop a politically inflected form of analysis. Discourse analysts are concerned with the internal structures of interactions in their immediate context, but are not overly concerned to relate these individual dialogues to larger social structures. A concern for the relation between the individual interaction and the wider discursive and social structure not only makes for a form of analysis which is more complex and more finely nuanced, but also makes for an analysis which is self-critical in terms of its own claims to 'truth', and is aware of the dangers of naively ascribing meaning to texts. It is this type of fusion of larger social questions with smaller-scale analytical questions which holds the greatest potential for future work in this field.

NOTES

1 A useful introduction to this type of discourse analysis, together with other analyst's work, is Brown and Yule (1983).

2 Formal linguistics is concerned largely with syntax (word order) and grammar (the structures and possibilities of combination of language items). Some also take formal linguistics to include a concern for semantics (word meaning). This type of study of language is at a fairly abstract level and is focused on the language system as a whole rather than particular utterances or particular texts. You might see it as concerned with Saussure's notion of *langue* (system) rather than *parole* (particular instances of language).

3 This labelling of discourse units has proved very helpful but it is also problematic: there seemed to be no particular justification for some of the labels chosen. As I point out later, the very fact of naming a discourse unit means that you have already decided that the unit has one particular function – you have therefore adopted a particular position in relation to that unit. Furthermore, whilst Sinclair and Coulthard in their early work developed a very limited number of terms to label discourse units, over time these terms proliferated, so that it became very difficult to decide which function a particular unit had. For more recent work in this area, see Coulthard (1992 and 1994) and Caldas-Coulthard and Coulthard (1996).

4 As well as being used by these analysts to refer to larger segments of text, composed of moves and exchanges, the term discourse is also

used by some linguists to refer to a particular type of language usage or to describe a particular grouping of texts which occur within a particular setting, for example, 'newspaper discourse', 'religious discourse', 'classroom discourse,' 'advertising discourse' (Cook, 1992). Here, it seems that the context of the production of the texts is what defines a discourse, and the term is here used almost interchangeably with words like 'genre'. This should not be confused with the Foucauldian definition of discourse, which is not limited to the context of production or the subject matter of a group of utterances. Nor should it be confused with the type of definition used by discourse analysts as a whole, where discourse is seen to mean a definable stretch of structured spoken or written text.

5   Certain linguists, such as Carmen Caldas-Coulthard and Deirdre Burton, have attempted to integrate a feminist analysis into discourse analysis, but their work tends to pull them more in the direction of the critical linguists, even though their definition of discourse is largely that of discourse analysis (Caldas-Coulthard, 1995; Caldas-Coulthard and Coulthard, 1996; Burton 1982).

6   Valentin Volosinov's work is also very useful in this context and has significantly influenced many of the critical linguists' work, since he starts from the premiss that language is not an expression of the self but rather that the social manifests itself in the individual conscious-ness through the vehicle of language. In this way, the values and ideologies of a society, embedded within the linguistic choices of the knowledge which is taken as self-evident within a culture, become the views and feelings of the individual, which that individual imagines are his/her own (Volosinov, 1973).

BIBLIOGRAPHY

Althusser, Louis (1984) *Essays on Ideology*, Verso, London.

Armstrong, Nancy and Tennenhouse, Leonard (eds) (1987) *The Ideology of Conduct: Essays in Literature and the History of Sexuality*, Methuen, London.

Ashcroft, Bill, Griffiths, Gareth and Tiffin, Helen (1989) *The Empire Writes Back: Theory and Practice in Post-Colonial Literatures*, Routledge, London.

Austin, John (1962) *How to do Things with Words*, Clarendon Press, Oxford.

Baldick, Chris (1983) *The Social Mission of English Criticism*, Oxford University Press, Oxford.

Baker-Miller, Jean (1978) *Towards a New Psychology of Women*, Penguin, Harmondsworth.

Bakshi, Parminder (1994) 'The politics of desire: E. M. Forster's encounters with India', in Davies, Tony and Wood, Nigel (eds) *A Passage to India: Theory in Practice*, Open University, Buckingham: 23–64.

Barthes, Roland (1986) 'The death of the author', in Barthes, *The Rustle of Language*, Blackwell, Oxford: 49–55.

—— (1990) *Fragments: A Lover's Discourse*, trans. Richard Howard, Penguin, London (first published 1977).

Bartky, Sandra (1988) 'Foucault, femininity and the modernization of patriarchal power', in Diamond, Irene and Quinby, Lee (eds) *Foucault and Feminism: Reflections of Resistance*, North Eastern University Press, Boston: 61–117.

Bate, Gavin (1992) 'Lessons in life', *Observer*, (supplement) June: 15.

Bell, David, Binnie, John, Cream, Julia, and Valentine, Gill (1994) 'All hyped up and no place to go', *Gender, Place and Culture: A Journal of Feminist Geography*, Vol.1, No.1: 31–34.

Belsey, Catherine (1980) *Critical Practice*, Methuen, London.

—— (1992) 'Materialist feminist criticism', paper given in the Gillian Skirrow Annual Lecture series, Strathclyde University, Glasgow.

Benveniste, Emile (1971) *Problems in General Linguistics*, University of Miami Press, Florida (first published 1966).

Bhabha, Homi (1994a) *The Location of Culture*, Routledge, London.

—— (1994b) 'Of mimicry and man: the ambivalence of colonial discourse', in Bhabha, *The Location of Culture*, Routledge, London: 85–93.

Brazil, David (1975) *Discourse Intonation*, Discourse Analysis Monographs I, English Language Research, University of Birmingham, Birmingham.

Brazil, David, Coulthard, Malcolm and Johns, Catherine (eds) (1980) *Discourse Intonation and Language Teaching*, Longman, Harlow.

Brown, Gillian and Yule, George (1983) *Discourse Analysis*, Cambridge University Press, Cambridge.

Brown, Penelope and Levinson, Stephen (1978) 'Universals in language usage: politeness phenomena', in Goody, Esther (ed.) *Questions and Politeness: Strategies in social interaction*, Cambridge University Press, Cambridge: 56–324.

Burton, Deirdre (1980) *Dialogue and Discourse: A Sociolinguistic Approach to Modern Drama Dialogue and Naturally Occurring Conversation*, Routledge & Kegan Paul, London.

—— (1982) 'Through dark glasses, through glass darkly', in Carter, Ronald (ed.), *Language and Literature*, Allen & Unwin, London: 195–214.

Butler, Judith (1990) *Gender Trouble: Feminism and the Subversion of Identity*, Routledge, London.

Caldas-Coulthard, Carmen (1995) 'Man in the news: the misrepresentation of women speaking in news-as-narrative-discourse,' in Mills, Sara (ed.) *Language and Gender: Interdisciplinary Perspectives*, Longman, Harlow: 226–240.

Caldas-Coulthard, Carmen and Coulthard, Malcolm (eds) (1996) *Texts and Practices: Readings in Critical Discourse Analysis*, Routledge, London.

Cameron, Deborah (ed.) (1990) *The Feminist Critique of Language: A Reader*, Routledge, London.

—— (1994) 'Words, words, words: the power of language', in Dunant, Sarah (ed.) *The War of the Words: The Political Correctness Debate*, Virago, London: 15–34.

Carrington, Dorothy (ed.) (1949) *The Traveller's Eye*, Pilot Press, London.

Carter, Ron and Simpson, Paul (eds) (1989) *Language, Discourse and Literature: An Introductory Reader in Discourse Stylistics*, Unwin Hyman, London.

Chakrabarty, Dipesh (1988) 'Conditions for knowledge of working-class conditions: employers, government and the jute workers of Calcutta, 1890–1940', in Guha, Ranajit and Spivak, Gayatri Chakravorty (eds) *Selected Subaltern Studies*, Oxford University Press, Oxford: 179–233.

Cliff, Tony (1984) *Class Struggle and Women's Liberation: 1640 to the Present Day*, Bookmarks, London.

Coates, Jennifer (1989) 'Gossip revisited: language in all-female groups', in Coates, J. and Cameron, D. (eds) *Women in their Speech Communities*, Longman, Harlow.

Coates, Jennifer and Cameron, Deborah (eds) (1989) *Women in their Speech Communities*, Longman, Harlow.

Collins Concise English Dictionary (1988) ed. Hanks, Patrick, Collins, Glasgow.

Collins Robert Concise French Dictionary (1990) ed. Atkins, Beryl *et al.*, Collins, Glasgow.

Cook, Guy (1992) *The Discourse of Advertising*, Routledge, London.

Coulthard, Malcolm (1977) *An Introduction to Discourse Analysis*, Longman, London.

—— (ed.) (1992) *Advances in Spoken Discourse Analysis*, Routledge, London.

—— (ed.) (1994) *Advances in Written Text Analysis*, Routledge, London.

Coulthard, Malcolm and Montgomery, Martin (eds) (1981) *Studies in Discourse Analysis*, Routledge & Kegan Paul, London.

Couzens Hoy, David (ed.) (1986) *Foucault: A Critical Reader*, Blackwell, Oxford.

Crowley, Tony (1989) *The Politics of Discourse: The Standard Language Question in British Cultural Debates*, Macmillan, London.

Crystal, David (1987) *The Cambridge Encyclopaedia of Language*, Cambridge University Press, Cambridge.

Darian-Smith, Kate, Gunner, Liz and Nuttall, Sarah (eds) (1996) *Text, Theory, Space: Land, Literature and History in South Africa and Australia*, Routledge, London.

David-Neel, Alexandra (1983) *My Journey to Lhasa*, Routledge, London.

Davis, Lennard (1983) *Factual Fictions: The Origins of the English Novel*, Columbia University Press, New York.

Diamond, Irene and Quinby, Lee (eds) (1988) *Foucault and Feminism: Reflections of Resistance*, North Eastern University Press, Boston.

Van Dijk, Teun, (ed.) (1985) *Handbook of Discourse Analysis: Volume 3, Discourse and Dialogue*, Academic Press, London and San Diego.

Doyle, Brian (1982) 'The hidden history of English studies', in Widdowson, P. (ed.) *Re-reading English*, Methuen, London: 17–31.

Dreyfus, Herbert and Rabinow, Paul (1982) *Michel Foucault: Beyond Structuralism and Hermeneutics*, Harvester, Brighton.

Dunant, Sarah (ed.) (1994) *The War of the Words: The Political Correctness Debate*, Virago, London.

Eagleton, Terry (1983) *Literary Theory: An Introduction*, Basil Blackwell, Oxford.

—— (1991) *Ideology: An Introduction*, Verso, London.

Eichenbaum, Luise and Orbach, Susie (1982) *Outside In: Inside Out – Women's Psychology: A Feminist Psychoanalytical Approach*, Pelican, Harmondsworth.

Fabian, Johannes (1983) *Time and the Other: How Anthropology Makes its Object*, Columbia University Press, New York.

Fairclough, Norman (1989) *Language and Power*, Longman, London.

—— (ed.) (1992a) *Critical Language Awareness*, Longman, Harlow.

—— (1992b) *Discourse and Social Change*, Polity, London.

—— (1995) *Media Discourse*, Edward Arnold, London.

Flint, Kate (1993) *The Woman Reader 1837–1914*, Clarendon Press, Oxford.

Forster, E. M. (1924) *A Passage to India* (1979 reprint), Penguin, Harmondsworth.

Foucault, Michel (1970) *The Order of Discourse: An Archaeology of the Human Sciences*, Tavistock, London.

—— (1972) *The Archaeology of Knowledge*, trans. Sheridan Smith, A. M., Tavistock, London (first published 1969)

—— (1977a) *Language, Counter-memory, Practice: Selected Essays and Interviews*, ed. Bouchard, D. F. and trans. Bouchard D. F. and Sherry, S., Blackwell, Oxford.

—— (1977b) 'The political function of the intellectual', *Radical Philosophy*, No. 17: 12–14.

—— (1978) *The History of Sexuality: An Introduction*, Vol. I, Penguin, Harmondsworth (first published 1972).

—— (1979a) *Discipline and Punish: The Birth of the Prison*, Vintage/Random House, New York.

—— (1979b) 'Interview with Lucette Finas', in Morris, Meaghan and Patton, Paul (eds) *Michel Foucault: Power/Truth/Strategy*, Feral Publications, Sydney: 67–75.

—— (1979c) 'The life of infamous men', in Morris, Meaghan and Patton, Paul (eds) *Michel Foucault: Power/Truth/Strategy*, Feral Publications, Sydney: 76–91.

—— (1979d). 'Powers and strategies: interview between Michel Foucault and Revoltes Logiques collective', in Morris, Meaghan and Patton, Paul (eds) *Michel Foucault: Power/Truth/Strategy*, Feral Publications, Sydney: 48–58.

—— (1979e) 'Truth and power: an interview with Alessandro Fontano and Pasquale Pasquino', in Morris, Meaghan and Patton, Paul (eds) *Michel Foucault: Power/Truth/Strategy*, Feral Publications, Sydney: 29–48.

—— (1980a) *Power/knowledge: Selected Interviews 1972–77*, ed. Gordon, C., Harvester, Brighton.

—— (1980b) 'What is an author?' in Harari, J. V. (ed.) *Textual Strategies: Perspectives in Post-structuralist Criticism*, Methuen, London.

—— (1981) 'The order of discourse', in Young, Robert (ed.) *Untying the Text: A Poststructuralist Reader*, RKP, London.

—— (1985) *The History of Sexuality: The Use of Pleasure*, Vol. II, Penguin, Harmondsworth (first published 1984).

Fowler, Roger (1981) *Language in the News: Discourse and Ideology in the Press*, Routledge, London.

Fowler, Roger, Hodge, Robert, Kress, Gunther and Trew, Tony (1979) *Language and Control*, Routledge & Kegan Paul, London.

Frow, John (1985) 'Discourse and power', in *Economy and Society*, Vol. 14, No. 2, May: 192–214.

Fuss, Diana (1990) *Essentially Speaking: Feminism, Nature and Difference*, Routledge, London.

Gilroy, Paul (1987) *There Ain't No Black in the Union Jack*, Routledge, London.

Graham, Elspeth, Hinds, Hilary, Hobby, Elaine and Wilcox, Helen (eds) (1989) *Her Own Life: Autobiographical Writings by Seventeenth Century Englishwomen*, Routledge, London.

Guha, Ranajit and Spivak, Gayatri Chakravorty (eds) (1988) *Selected Subaltern Studies*, Oxford University Press, New York.

Hacking, Ian (1986) 'The archaeology of Foucault', in Couzens Hoy, D. (ed.) *Foucault: A Critical Reader*, Blackwell, Oxford: 27–40.

Hanbury-Tenison, Robin (ed.) (1993) *The Oxford Book of Exploration*, Oxford University Press, Oxford.

Hawthorn, Jeremy (1992) *A Concise Glossary of Contemporary Literary Theory*, Edward Arnold, London.

Hennessy, Rosemary (1993) *Materialist Feminism and the Politics of Discourse*, Routledge, London.

Hobby, Elaine (1988) *Virtue of Necessity: English Women's Writing 1649–1688*, Virago, London.

Hodge, Robert and Kress, Gunther (1988) *Social Semiotics*, Polity, London.

Hoey, Michael (1983) *On the Surface of Discourse*, Allen & Unwin, London.

Holmes, Janet (1995) *Women, Men and Politeness*, Longman, Harlow.

Hulme, Peter (1986) *Colonial Encounters: Europe and the Native Caribbean 1492–1797*, Methuen, London.

Jones, Peter (1996) 'Academic jargon: how to publish it', *The Times*, 25 May: 16.

Laclau, Ernesto and Mouffe, Chantal (1985) *Hegemony and Socialist Strategy: Towards a Radical Democratic Politics*, trans. Moore, Winston and Cammack, Paul, Verso, London.

Landry, Donna and MacLean, Gerald (1993) *Materialist Feminisms*, Blackwell, Oxford.

Laws, Sophie (1990) *Issues of Blood: The Politics of Menstruation*, Macmillan, Basingstoke.

Lee, David (1992) *Competing Discourses: Perspective and Ideology in Language*, Longman, Harlow.

Longman Dictionary of the English Language (1984) ed. Gay, Heather *et al.*, Longman, Harlow.

Lovell, Terry (1980) *Pictures of Reality: Aesthetics, Politics and Pleasure*, BFI, London.

Lovering, Kathryn Matthews (1995) 'The bleeding body: adolescents talk about menstruation', in Wilkinson, Sue and Kitzinger, Celia (eds) *Feminism and Discourse*, Sage, London: 10–31.

Low, Gail Ching-Liang (1996) *White Skin Black Masks: Representation and Colonialism*, Routledge, London.

McClintock, Anne (1995) *Imperial Leather: Race, Gender and Sexuality in the Imperial Contest*, Routledge, London.

Macdonnell, Diane (1986) *Theories of Discourse*, Blackwell, Oxford.

Macey, David (1993) *The Lives of Michel Foucault*, Verso, London.

Macmillan, Margaret (1988) *Women of the Raj*, Thames & Hudson, London.

McNay, Lois (1992) *Foucault and Feminism*, Polity Press, Oxford.

Mey, Jacob (1993) *Pragmatics: An Introduction*, Blackwell, Oxford.

Mills, Sara (1991) *Discourses of Difference: Women's Travel Writing and Colonialism*, Routledge, London.

—— (1992a) 'Discourse competence: or how to theorise strong women speakers', *Hypatia*, Vol. 7, No. 2, Spring: 4–17.

—— (1992b) 'Negotiating discourses of femininity', *Journal of Gender Studies*, Vol. 1, No. 3, May: 271–285.

—— (ed.) (1994a) *Gendering the Reader*, Harvester Wheatsheaf, Hemel Hempstead.

—— (1994b) 'Knowledge, gender and empire', in Blunt, Alison and Rose, Gillian (eds) *Writing Women and Space: Colonial and Post-colonial Geographies*, Guilford, New York: 29–50.

—— (1994c) 'Representing the unrepresentable: Alice Jardine's *Gynesis* and E. M. Forster's *A Passage to India*', in Davies, Tony and Wood, Nigel (eds) *A Passage to India: Theory in Practice*, Open University Press, Buckingham: 121–143.

—— (1995a) 'Discontinuity and post-colonial discourse', *Ariel: A Review of International English Literature*, Vol. 26, No. 3, July: 73–88.

—— (1995b) *Feminist Stylistics*, Routledge, London.

—— (ed.) (1995c) *Language and Gender: Interdisciplinary Perspectives*, Longman, Harlow.

—— (1996a) 'Colonial domestic space', *Renaissance and Modern Studies*, special issue on gender and space, Vol. 39: 46–60.

—— (1996b) 'Gender and colonial space', *Gender, Place and Culture*, Vol. 3, No. 2: 125–147.

—— (1996c) 'Post-colonial feminist theory', in Mills, Sara and Pearce, Lynne (eds) *Feminist Readings/Feminists Reading*, Harvester Wheatsheaf, Hemel Hempstead: 257–279.

—— (1996d) 'Powerful talk', unpublished discussion paper, Loughborough University.

Mills, Sara and Pearce, Lynne (eds) (1996) *Feminists Reading/Feminist Readings* (2nd, revised, edition), Harvester Wheatsheaf, Hemel Hempstead.

Mills, Sara and White, Christine (forthcoming) 'Discursive categories and desire', in Harvey, K. and Shalom, C. (eds) *Language and Desire*, Routledge, London.

Moi, Toril (ed.) (1986) *The Kristeva Reader*, Blackwell, Oxford.

Morris, James (1979a) *Heaven's Command: An Imperial Progress*, Penguin, Harmondsworth.

—— (1979b) *Farewell the Trumpets: An Imperial Retreat*, Penguin, Harmondsworth.

—— (1979c) *Pax Britannica: The Climax of an Empire*, Penguin, Harmondsworth.

Morris, Meaghan (1979) 'The pirate's fiancée', in Morris, Meaghan and Patton, Paul (eds) *Michel Foucault: Power/Truth/Strategy*, Feral Publications, Sydney: 148–168.

—— (1989) *The Pirate's Fiancée*, Verso, London.

Morris, Meaghan and Patton, Paul (eds) (1979) *Michel Foucault: Power/Truth/Strategy*, Feral Publications, Sydney.

Palmer, Paulina (1989) *Contemporary Women's Fiction*, Harvester, Hemel Hempstead.

Patton, Paul (1979) 'Of power and prisons', in Morris, Meaghan and Patton, Paul (eds) *Michel Foucault: Power/Truth/Strategy*, Feral Publications, Sydney: 109–146.

Pecheux, Michel (1982) *Language, Semantics and Ideology*, Macmillan, Basingstoke (first published in French in 1975).

Porter, Bernard (1968) *Critics of Empire: British Radical Attitudes to Colonialism in Africa, 1895–1914*, Macmillan, London.

Porter, Dennis (1982) 'Orientalism and its problems', in Barker, F. (ed.) *The Politics of Theory*, Proceedings of the Essex Sociology of Literature Conference, University of Essex, Colchester.

Poster, Mark (1984) *Foucault, Marxism and History: Mode of Production vs. Mode of Information*, Polity Press, London.

Potter, Jonathan and Wetherell, Margaret (1987) *Discourse and Social Psychology: Beyond Attitudes and Behaviour*, Sage, London.

Pratt, Mary Louise (1985) 'Scratches on the face of the country: or what Mr. Barrows saw in the land of the Bushmen', *Critical Inquiry*, Vol. 12, No.1, Autumn: 119–143.

—— (1992) *Imperial Eyes: Travel Writing and Transculturation*, Routledge, London.

Rabinow, Paul (ed.) (1984) *The Foucault Reader*, Penguin, Harmondsworth.

Richards, Thomas (1993) *The Imperial Archive: Knowledge and the Fantasy of Empire*, Verso, London.

Said, Edward (1978) *Orientalism*, Routledge & Kegan Paul, London.

—— (1993) *Culture and Imperialism*, Chatto & Windus, London.

Sawicki, Jana (1991) *Disciplining Foucault: Feminism, Power and the Body*, Routledge, London and New York.

Searle, John (1979) *Speech Acts*, Cambridge University Press, Cambridge.

Sharpe, Jenny (1993) *Allegories of Empire: The Figure of Woman in the Colonial Text*, University of Minnesota Press, Minneapolis.

Sheridan, Alan (1980) *Michel Foucault: The Will to Truth*, Tavistock, London.

Showalter, Elaine (1977) *A Literature of their Own: British Women Novelists from Bronte to Lessing*, Princeton University Press, Princeton.

—— (1987) *The Female Malady: Women, Madness and English Culture*, Virago, London.

Shuttle, Penelope and Redgrove, Peter (1978) *The Wise Wound: Menstruation and Everywoman*, Gollancz, London.

Sinclair, John and Coulthard, Malcolm (1975) *Towards an Analysis of Discourse: The English Used by Pupils and Teachers*, Oxford University Press, Oxford.

Smart, Barry (1985) *Michel Foucault*, Tavistock, London.

Smith, Dorothy (1990) *Texts, Facts and Femininity: Exploring the Relations of Ruling*, Routledge, London.

Spender, Dale (1980) *Man Made Language*, RKP, London.

Spivak, Gayatri Chakravorty (1988) *In Other Worlds: Essays in Cultural Politics*, Routledge, London.

—— (1990) *The Post-Colonial Critic: Interviews, Strategies, Dialogues*, ed. Sarah Harasym, Routledge, London.

—— (1993a) 'Can the subaltern speak?', in Williams, Patrick and Chrisman, Laura (eds) *Colonial Discourse and Post-colonial Theory*, Harvester Wheatsheaf, Hemel Hempstead: 66–111.

—— (1993b) *Outside in the Teaching Machine*, Routledge, London.

—— (1995) 'Three women's texts and a critique of imperialism', in Ashcroft, Bill, Griffiths, Gareth, and Tiffin, Helen (eds) *The Post-colonial Studies Reader*, Routledge, London: 269–273.

Steel, Flora Annie and Gardiner, Grace (1891) *The Complete Indian Housekeeper and Cook*, Heinemann, London, (first published 1888).

Stubbs, Michael (1983) *Discourse Analysis: The Sociolinguistic Analysis of Natural Language*, Blackwell, Oxford.

Sunderland, Jane (ed.) (1994) *Exploring Gender: Questions and Implications for English Language Education*, Prentice Hall, Hemel Hempstead.

Tannen, Deborah (1990) *You Just Don't Understand: Women and Men in Conversation*, William Morrow, New York.

Taylor, Charles (1986) 'Foucault on freedom and truth', in Couzens Hoy, D. (ed.) *Foucault: A Critical Reader*, Blackwell, Oxford.

Threadgold, Terry (1988) 'Stories of race and gender: an unbounded discourse' , in Birch, D. and O'Toole, M. (eds) *Functions of Style*, Pinter, London.

—— (1997) *Feminist Poetics: Poetics, Performance, Histories*, Routledge, London.

Trew, Tony (1979a) 'Theory and ideology at work', in Fowler, R. *et al.*, *Language and Control*, Routledge & Kegan Paul, London: 94–116.

—— (1979b) 'What the papers say: linguistic variation and ideological difference', in Fowler, R. *et al.*, *Language and Control*, Routledge & Kegan Paul, London: 117–156.

Vetterling-Braggin, M. (ed.) (1981) *Sexist Language: a Modern Philosophical Analysis*, Littlefield Adams, Totowa, N.J.

Vice, Sue (ed.) (1996) *Psychoanalytic Criticism: A Reader*, Polity, London.

Voloshinov, Valentin (1973) *Marxism and the Philosophy of Language*, trans. Matejka, L. and Titunik, I., Seminar Press, New York (first published 1930).

Walby, Sylvia (1990) *Theorizing Patriarchy*, Blackwell, Oxford.

Walzer Michael (1986) 'The politics of Michel Foucault', in Couzens Hoy, D. (ed.) *Foucault: A Critical Reader*, Blackwell, Oxford: 51–68.

Wetherell, Margaret and Potter, Jonathan (1992) *Mapping the Language of Racism: Discourse and the Legitimation of Exploitation*, Harvester Wheatsheaf, Hemel Hempstead.

Whitehead, Neil (ed.) (forthcoming) *Walter Ralegh's Discoverie of the Beautiful Empire of Guyana*, Exploring Travel Series, Manchester University Press, Manchester.

Wilkinson, Sue (1986) *Feminist Social Psychology*, Open University Press, Milton Keynes.

Wilkinson, Sue and Kitzinger, Celia (eds) (1995) *Feminism and Discourse: Psychological Perspectives*, Sage, London.

Williams, Patrick and Chrisman, Laura (eds) (1993) *Colonial Discourse and Post-colonial Theory: A Reader*, Harvester Wheatsheaf, Hemel Hempstead.

Young, Robert (1995) *Colonial Desire: Hybridity, Theory, Culture and Race*, Routledge, London.

INDEX

access to discourse 14, 97–9
agency 30, 42, 85, 91, 93, 102, 122
Althusser, Louis 11, 32, 34, 38, 43
ambivalence 124, 154
archaeology 26, 49, 61, 75, 85
archive 49, 63
Austen, Jane 74
Austin, John 28, 61
author 72–5
author-fiction 74

Bacon, Francis 74
Baikie, William 109, 112
Baker-Miller, Jean 83, 87
Bakhtin, Mikhail 7, 9, 11
Bakshi, Parminder 127
Baldick, Chris 25
Balibar, Renee 14
Barrow, John 115
Barthes, Roland 9, 48–9, 55–6, 72, 75
Bartky, Sandra 94
Bate, Gavin 111
Bell, David 92
Belsey, Catherine 59
Bhabha, Homi 106, 111, 123, 124–5, 126
Binnie, Jonh 92
Benveniste, Emile 4–5, 9
Brazil, David 132, 142
Broadhurst, Thomas 89
Brown, Gillian 138–40
Burton, Deirdre 132, 139, 159
Butler, Judith 102–3

Caldas-Coulthard, Carmen 159

Cameron, Deborah 45, 97, 98
capitalism 36
Chakrabarty, Dipesh 121
class 78–9
Cliff, Tony 78
Coates, Jennifer 97, 98
colonialism 100, 101, 129
colonial discourse 10, 22, 27, 105–30
commentary 67–8
competitive strategies 98–9
confessional 80–6
Conrad, Joseph 101
contact zone 121
cooperative strategies 98–9
Coulthard, Malcolm 132, 136, 138, 139, 141, 154
Cream, Julia 92
critical linguistics 9, 10, 27, 131–59
critical theory 8
critique 32–3
Crystal, David 3–4
cultural theory 8, 10

Dampier, William 114
Darian-Smith, Kate 119, 125
David-Neel, Alexandra 100–1
Davis, Lennard 66
Diamond, Irene 77
discipline 69, 80–1, 94–5
discontinuity 26, 59
discours 2, 6
discourse analysis 10, 27, 131–59
discourse markers 136
discourse theory 16, 33, 77–104, 147–57

discursive constraints 51, 86, 96
discursive field 50
discursive formation 49
discursive frameworks 33, 49, 106
discursive structures 12–15, 17–18,
    48–76, 85–6, 89, 97, 115, 149,
    154
disidentification 15
dominant discourse 19
Doyle, Brian 25
Dreyfus, Herbert 28, 60–1
Dunant, Sarah 43

Eagleton, Terry 25, 32, 46
Eichenbaum, Luise 83
episteme 56–60
ethnographic present 112
ethnomethodology 152
exclusion 12, 24–5, 63–7

Fabian, Johannes 111–14
Fairclough, Norman 10, 18, 46, 134,
    137, 141, 142, 148, 149, 150–7
false consciousness 32–3, 43
femininity 80, 86–93
feminist theory 10, 12, 42, 68,
    77–104
Flint, Kate 89–90
Forster, E.M. 126
Foucault, Michel 6–7, 8, 10, 13,
    16–22, 30–47, 48–76, 77, 78, 79,
    81, 85, 90, 95, 103, 106, 122, 132,
    134, 143, 145, 148, 149, 150, 154,
    157
Fountaine, Margaret 116
Fowler, Roger 6, 134, 148
Frow, John 19, 50
Fuss, Diana 102–3

Gardiner, Grace 116

genealogy 35
Gilroy, Paul 108
Gramsci, Antonio 105
Guha, Ranajit 42, 120

Hacking, Ian 26
Hawthorn, Jeremy 4
hegemony 30, 104, 154
Hennessy, Rosemary 46
heterosexuality 86–93
Hindess, Barry 10
Hirst, Paul 10
histoire 5
history 26
Hodge, Robert 134, 148
Hoey, Michael 132, 135, 139
Holmes, Janet 41
Hulme, Peter 105, 106, 117–19, 126

ideology 4, 6, 27, 29–47, 54, 78,
    86, 91, 100, 157
imperialism 106, 129
intertextuality 153–5

Jones, Peter 72

Kingsley, Mary 116
Kitzinger Celia 132, 146–7
knowledge 22, 53, 58, 75, 109,
    115–16, 122, 132, 146, 149, 152
Kress, Gunther 134, 148
Kristeva, Julia 153–4

Laclau, Ernesto 50
language 42–6, 133
Lawrence T E 119
Laws, Sophie 12
Leech, Geoffrey 4
linguistics 9, 10, 131–59
literary texts 73

literary theory 8
literature 22–7
Low, Gail Ching-Liang 124
Lovell, Terry 51

Macdonnell, Diane 10–12, 42, 56, 73
Macey, David 30
Macmillan, Margaret 65
Martin, Biddy 88
Marxist 26, 27, 29–32, 34–6, 38, 39, 42, 54, 59, 60, 78, 134
Matthews Lovering, Kathryn 146
McNay, Lois 77
Mey, Jacob 142
mimicry 124
Moi, Toril 34
Montgomery, Martin 132
Morris, James 108
Morris, Meaghan 78
Mouffe, Chantal 50

non-discursive 54
North, Marianne 116

objects 52
Othering 106–18, 125
Orbach, Susie 83

Palmer, Paulina 87
patriarchy 93, 95
Patton, Paul 36
Pearce, Lynne 103
Pecheux, Michel 10–11, 13–15, 150
political 77, 79–80, 105, 133, 148, 157
political correctness 43, 45
Polo, Marco 119
Porter, Bernard 122
Porter, Dennis 119, 122

post-colonial discourse 10, 105–30
post-colonial theory 27, 42, 105–30
postmodern 59
postmodernism 76
post-structuralism 8, 34, 56, 76, 132, 143, 146
Potter, Jonathan 132, 133, 143–7
power 10, 17–20, 36–9, 78, 88, 93–4, 98, 133, 142, 145, 152, 154
power/knowledge 21–2, 23
Pratt, Mary Louise 53, 105, 108, 115, 116, 121, 126
psychoanalysis 34, 102, 123–9

Quinby, Lee 77

Rabinow, Paul 28, 60–1
race 78–9
racism 9, 44, 108, 133, 143–7
rarefaction 70
real 49–53
Redgrove, Peter 13
repressive hypothesis 19, 37, 39
resistance 42, 116, 128
rhetoric 145–6
Richards, Thomas 109

Said, Edward 105, 106, 107, 108, 113, 116, 117, 119, 120, 126, 129, 130
Sawicki, Jana 77
Searle, John 28, 61
sexism 9, 43–6
Sharpe, Jenny 123
Short, Michael 4
Showalter, Elaine 69, 81
Shuttle, Penelope 12
Sinclair, John 136, 139, 141, 154
Smith, Dorothy 77, 82, 85, 86, 87, 91–3

social psychology 9, 27, 131–59
Sokal, Alan 72
speech acts 61, 67
Spender, Dale 43–4, 98
Spivak, Gayatri 42, 106, 120
statement 6, 13, 27–8, 32–3, 48, 56, 60–1, 62, 66
Steel, Flora Annie 116
structuralist 8, 49, 75
structures 7, 12, 48–76
Stubbs, Michael 4
subaltern 120
subject 33–5, 42, 102–3
subject-in-crisis 34
Sunderland, Jane 43

Tannen, Deborah 97
Taylor, Charles 26, 50
text 3, 4, 49, 133
text analysis 3, 133, 140, 157
Thornton, Alice 83

Threadgold, Terry 134
Trew, Tony 134, 148
truth 18–19, 32–3, 66, 69, 84, 146, 158

Valentine, Gill 92
Vetterling-Braggin, Mary 43
Vice, Sue 34
Volosinov, Valentin 11, 159

Walby, Sylvia 93
Wallace, Alfred 117
Walzer, Michael 26
Wetherell, Margaret 132, 133, 143–7
White, Christine 96
Whitehead, Neil 121
Wilkinson, Sue 83, 132, 146–7
will to truth 66–7

Young, Robert 58, 108, 123
Yule, George 138–9